HOUSEPLANTS
FOR FREE

A Step-by-Step Guide To The Propagation Of
Healthy Houseplants

KEN MARCH

CHARTWELL
BOOKS, INC.

A QUINTET BOOK

Published by Chartwell Books
A Division of Book Sales, Inc.
110 Enterprise Avenue
Secaucus, New Jersey 07094

ISBN 1-55521-297-2

This book was designed and produced by
Quintet Publishing Limited
6 Blundell Street
London N7 9BH

Art Director: Peter Bridgewater
Designer: Annie Moss
Editors: Shaun Barrington, Geraldine Christie
Photographer: Paul Forrester

Typeset in Great Britain by
Central Southern Typesetters, Eastbourne
Manufactured in Hong Kong by
Regent Publishing Services Limited
Printed in Hong Kong by
South Sea Int'l Press Ltd.

Contents

*T*he idea of being able to produce plants for free sounds too good to be true, almost like growing money on trees. While not quite so simple, with a little effort and an informed approach you can achieve rewarding results.

Although the propagation techniques described in this book are based on techniques used to propagate the many varieties of houseplants cultivated by commercial growers, it has to be remembered that propagating a cutting is just the start of the process. Painstaking skill and cultural care need to follow to grow quality houseplants.

Once you have experimented with propagating and experienced the fun that comes with producing plants, you can develop your skills to try to produce plants of the quality that are grown commercially. First, however, you need to know when and how to propagate them.

WHEN TO PROPAGATE

*A*lthough theoretically many plants can be commercially propagated throughout the year, in the home one tends to be limited mostly to the spring and summer.

Commercial growers use sophisticated methods of environmental control to provide the correct temperature, level of humidity and even light and day-length control. In the home, therefore, you need to make maximum use of the times of the year when environmental conditions are more conducive to gaining greater success.

Apart from making best use of the spring and summer when ambient temperatures are higher and usually more stable, the improved light levels with longer hours of daylight are particularly important. Rooting or propagating the plant is not enough for, once propagated, it is important to build on the success and produce a well-formed healthy plant.

Propagating a plant at the right time and early enough in the season will provide sufficient time to grow on the plant ready to endure some of the traumas of the winter. Conversely, propagating a plant too late in the season can lead to all sorts of problems. Even if the plant is propagated and rooted successfully late in the season, if it has not grown and become established sufficiently the growth can weaken and etiolate, leaving the plant more susceptible to disease. The new plant is weak and can easily succumb to low temperatures, too much water, temperature fluctuations or even draughts, even if disease is kept at bay. It is, therefore, imperative that the health of the plant is maintained to avoid disappointment.

Equally important is the fact that, apart from the choice of the right time of the year, the right plant must also be selected. Never propagate from a sickly or diseased plant. Also check that the plant to be propagated is free from pests. It is better to eliminate the pest or disease problem before propagation, as plants treated during propagation are usually more susceptible to loss or damage than when they are growing actively.

EQUIPMENT

*A*lthough the simplest method of propagation
may only require a glass jar of water, it is
worth considering what equipment you may
need to propagate many types of plants by different
methods.

Fortunately, the range of tools required is relatively basic, with the greatest emphasis on *cutting implements*. Apart from a sharp knife, you may find a surgical scalpel useful for delicate cutting operations which require a very sharp and precise cutting technique, such as making delicate and intricate operations when grafting.

Sharp tools are really the key to the start of a successful propagation sequence and this is equally important when applied to even a basic tool like scissors. You may find vine scissors useful, otherwise a sturdy domestic pair with sharp blades that do not flex apart may be adequate.

For larger and tougher stemmed subjects a pair of secateurs or pruning shears is an important and indispensable tool. However, it is preferable not to use the type that consists of a sharp blade cutting onto an anvil, as these may bruise tissue, leading to possible loss of the cutting by allowing a disease organism to enter the plant through the wound. If possible, use the type with two cutting blades or with a sharp blade that cuts against an anvil in a scissor action.

Another useful tool is a small piece of stick or wooden rod to *dibble* holes into the compost before cuttings are inserted; this helps to avoid any damage that can occur to soft, succulent tissue on varieties such as African violet (saintpaulia). It also helps to prevent loss of the rooting powder as the cutting is inserted into a ready-made hole with the powder still covering the base of the stem.

Apart from a selection of *pots* comprising 2½in (6cm), 3½in (9cm), 4¼in (11cm) and 5in (13cm), and a 5½in (14cm) half-pot or pan, a most useful tool is a *heated propagation unit* in which pots or trays can be propagated.

However, these can be expensive as the most sophisticated units also feature mist systems. If the concept of plants for free is to be achieved it is perhaps advisable to develop one's skills and experience first before incurring the capital expenditure.

An improvement over a basic clear plastic bag to cover the cuttings is the use of a bell jar or a basic plastic propagator consisting of a seed tray with a clear plastic cover which may be vented by simple louvre adjustments.

Probably the most basic, but also most popular, method of improving humidity, however, is a *clear plastic bag*. To make best use of it, provide some support in the form of sticks or canes to hold the bag up and away from contact with the plant being propagated. Corks fitted on to the

ABOVE LEFT *Some of the basic equipment needed for propagation: a selection of pots, watering can, maximum-minimum thermometer, canes and mister.*

ABOVE *Seed tray with vented plastic lid (left) and the more sophisticated kind of propagator (right) incorporating a heated element.*

LEFT *The simplest, unheated propagator; inexpensive and quite adequate as a starting point for the inexperienced.*

■ EQUIPMENT ■

tops of the sticks will render them safer to work with. Alternatively, a piece of strong wire bent into a hoop will also work.

Another useful item is an *anti-transpirant spray* similar to that used on Christmas trees to help prevent needle drop. Although not essential, it can be used to advantage on some plants to reduce water loss. Alternatively, a small hand mister may be used on cuttings that respond well to mist, such as poinsettia.

Before inserting the cutting into compost dip it into a *hormone rooting powder*. This material helps to accelerate the cutting's production of roots by stimulating the area at the base of the stem.

Although an enormous range of recipes for *compost* exist, with special mixes for almost every type of cutting, it is quite impractical to mix your own unless you are a real enthusiast. It is difficult to produce the correct structure and absolutely right balance of nutrients which are critical for the plant's early development. It is, therefore, better to use proprietary composts that are specially blended for the appropriate purpose, such as seed and cutting compost for germinating seeds and striking cuttings. Cacti and succulents compost may be used where appropriate for these specialized plants and a peat-based potting compost can often help to develop a fibrous root system more rapidly than heavier soil-based composts.

The latter may be used later in the plant's development if preferred.

As an alternative to striking a cutting in either water or compost you might like to consider the use of a *rooting gel*. A wide range of cuttings may be struck in the material before being potted up and grown on.

Finally, a *maximum–minimum thermometer* is very useful for recording the temperature of a particular environment to allow an accurate check of highs and lows, especially when a more even temperature is called for.

Safety should be considered at all times and, although it is basic common sense, you remember to keep all tools and materials out of the way of children at *all* times. The danger of sharp knives, secateurs, pruning shears and chemicals may be obvious to you but may not be to a child. Also bear in mind that plastic bags are extremely dangerous and should never be left lying around.

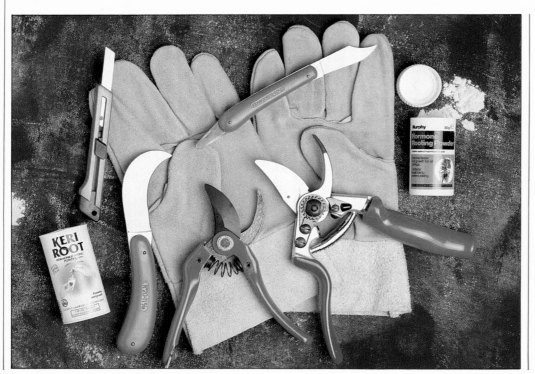

ABOVE LEFT *Hormone rooting powder will encourage the production of roots, particularly in those plants which have woody stems. Some brands contain fungicide which helps to prevent stem rot.*

LEFT *Hormone rooting powders, leather gloves (far more effective for most jobs than cotton or rubber) and (from left to right) the cutting edge of successful propagation: scalpel (X-Acto knife), pruning knife, small pruners, budding knife, and secateurs.*

■ ENVIRONMENTAL CONTROL ■

To be effective at propagation, whether by germinating seed, striking cuttings or grafting, it is absolutely essential to be able to control the environment around the plant.

TEMPERATURE

While a reasonable temperature is vital, it is more important to aim for a stable temperature rather than to try to raise the level too high during the day, then allow it to drop dramatically overnight. Temperature fluctuation can be a major problem, especially during the early stages of propagation.

Whenever possible, ensure that the temperature suggested for propagating is aimed for with little variance above or below. For this reason alone late spring and early summer offer a more stable environment for plants in the home.

Temperatures are likely to fluctuate from late autumn to early spring as the home is heated when people are active and then usually allowed to cool when they have retired to bed.

The success of propagation depends to a large extent upon the temperature being controlled correctly, but for the greatest number of plants this should not be too much of a problem and can be achieved by careful siting. However, there are some plants that need a much higher temperature to root or germinate, when a temperature of 80°F (27°C) may be required. This may be particularly difficult to achieve unless you can find a position close to a solid-fuel boiler or you manage to time the operation to coincide with a heat wave. For these more difficult plants it may be worth considering purchasing a heated propagation unit – but only if you are keen and will make full use of it. Otherwise, try harder to find a situation in the home that

may fulfil the temperature requirement. Greater success with propagating may be achieved by trying to aim for a soil temperature slightly higher than the air temperature, by about 5°F (2–3°C).

A maximum–minimum thermometer, recording the highest and lowest temperatures, will initially help you find the best position as far as temperature is required.

HUMIDITY

Humidity is another important factor to consider, especially as a cutting with a thin leaf will lose more water when the atmosphere is warm and dry rather than when it is warm and humid.

All plants lose water by a process called transpiration. Some plants, such as cacti and other succulents, lose water very slowly and, indeed, some of the thicker, waxy-leaved plants do likewise. For these, water loss is not much of a problem and you need not worry about controlling the humidity.

However, for the greatest number of plants that you may wish to propagate, water loss and low humidity can be a real problem and a major cause of early failure is due to rapid dehydration. This may have started as soon as the cutting was taken and its water supply disrupted.

There are two main ways in which the likelihood of this happening may be lessened.

First, the relatively few cuttings that may be struck in water first are less likely to suffer because their supply of water is of course more readily available than if they were simply inserted in compost. The use of a rooting gel also helps to alleviate the problem to a large extent, because of the material's extremely high water content.

A second method of reducing water loss and attempting to maintain the cutting in a turgid, rather than flaccid, state is to place some sort of barrier over the leaf surface. This can be done by various means: spraying and misting is used widely by commercial horticulturalists, but the use of plastic bags (also used commercially) is probably more practical in the home.

Spraying cuttings with an anti-transpirant mist, similar to that used on Christmas trees to reduce needle drop (again the result of dehydration in a warm room), helps to reduce water loss by the natural process of transpiration. Be sure to get an even cover over the leaves. This type of spray may be of benefit to a wide range of plants, but really is of major benefit where the plant to be propagated is vulnerable to too much moisture in its environment.

▮ ENVIRONMENTAL CONTROL ▮

A further way of reducing water loss is by misting the cuttings regularly with tepid, never cold, water. This helps in two ways: it covers the leaves with a barrier of water that not only reduces water loss by physically coating the leaves, but also evaporates to the atmosphere, thereby helping to improve the relative humidity.

To be effective, misting with water needs to be done regularly and often much more than once or twice a day. Some cuttings may need to be misted as much as once every ten to fifteen minutes during hot, dry sunny spells. When they are propagated commercially, and even in the home during similar conditions, you may need to mist once an hour or so.

The use of a small hand mister may be sufficient if you can keep up with the requirements of the cuttings, always trying to avoid their flagging by misting before it happens. However, if you are really keen and can justify the expense, sophisticated propagation units are available with not only an in-built temperature control but also a mist unit which can be programmed to suit. Probably the easiest method of improving the humidity, reducing water loss and providing a more stable environment is to create a microclimate around your cuttings. Simply covering your cuttings with a physical barrier such as a glass dome or plastic bag will reduce water loss to the surrounding atmosphere and improve the level within the enclosed space.

Ficus pumila: dehydration of leaves due to lack of water.

A clear plastic bag is probably the simplest item to use and this can be placed over the pot and cuttings and kept open to avoid contact with the leaves with a small frame. A piece of plastic-covered or galvanized wire can be bent into a hoop or upside down 'U' shape and inserted in the pot to hang the bag over. Alternatively, small sticks, preferably with corks on the end to help prevent any accidents, may be inserted in the pot to support the bag.

Occasionally it may be necessary to remove the bag if it becomes too wet, to avoid the conditions becoming more beneficial to the growth and spread of pathogenic fungal rots, rather than the rapid striking of cuttings.

Croton: excessive wilting probably caused by root loss due to over-watering.

Whatever you use as a cover, do remember to place a tray or some other barrier underneath as water vapour will condense on the inside of the bag and run down on to whatever it touches.

Either a plastic bag or a jar can be used to maintain high humidity. Ensure that the covering does not touch the cutting.

LIGHT

Finally, the other key element of environmental control is light; without it, plants will not grow.

Generally speaking, cuttings of plants being propagated require a similar, but perhaps slightly less, amount of light than a plant growing normally. Try whenever possible to provide cuttings of a plant being propagated with the correct level for the type of plant. For example, a croton or codiaeum will require much more light than a maranta.

However, even for plants that normally have a high light requirement, take care to ensure that they are not exposed to direct sunlight. Young cuttings are extremely susceptible to damage, especially from leaf scorch. A bathroom, with its diffused light and humidity, can be ideal, provided that it is not too dark or cold.

At the other extreme, cuttings given too little light will stretch and become very weak, resulting in probable loss or at the very least a sickly and poor plant to grow on. Spindly plants rarely grow into strong and healthy specimens.

BASIC TECHNIQUES OF PROPAGATION

*T*he various ways that plants can be propagated are diverse, offering the enthusiast considerable scope for developing his or her skills. Although the basic techniques are generally straightforward, and only require minor modification to suit specific needs, it is important initially to understand the basics before becoming too adventurous.

SEED

*S*eed sowing is possibly the most common method of propagation and a way by which many more plants can be raised than by other methods. There are, however, a number of disadvantages, not least of which is the fact that with certain plants, young plants raised from seed will not come true to the parent, presenting the raiser with an array of the plant's mixed parentage. Plants raised from seed may also take longer than those raised from cuttings.

For the best results when sowing seed, use a clean seed-tray or half-pot and lightly fill it with seed and cutting compost. Do not compress the compost, particularly if it is peat based, but gently level it by tamping just sufficiently to produce a flat surface to sow on to.

If the seed to be sown is very fine, as in the case of fern spores or begonia seed, the compost should be watered first. This may be done with a watering can fitted with a fine rose or, alternatively, by gently immersing the compost in a bowl of water, not quite letting the level of the water rise over the compost surface.

The fine seed should then be thinly sown in a careful zigzag pattern, first in one direction and then at a right angle to it. Once sown, the seed should then be germinated as suggested for the type of houseplant.

If, however, the seed is larger and more visible, it may be sown prior to watering, sprinkling the seed with a layer of compost just sufficient to cover it evenly. Lightly watering the seed with a watering can fitted with a fine rose will then settle the compost gently, provided that it is not done so clumsily as to dislodge the seed.

Subsequent waterings may be carried out by either partial immersion, watering with a fine rose or by even spraying with a hand-held plant mister which has the advantage of supplying a level of water in a light and controllable fashion.

Lightly fill pot with seed and cutting compost.

Thinly sow seed, tapping folded paper or envelope to sprinkle evenly.

Gently level compost to avoid any air spaces, but do not compact.

Evenly cover seed with compost and lightly water.

PRICKING OUT SEEDLINGS

*O*nce the seed has germinated and is large enough to be pricked out, the new plants are very vulnerable. Care should be taken not to damage the tender young seedlings.

First, the compost should be evenly watered – not saturated – and then the seedlings carefully lifted and, where necessary, separated. Take care not to crush or bruise the tender stems, but to hold the seedlings gently by their leaves.

A hole should be dibbled into the pot into which the seedling is to be potted and the roots carefully dropped in. Once the level of the seedling is adjusted to the correct height, push compost lightly around the stem to support the young plant.

BASIC TECHNIQUES OF PROPAGATION

Never firm a seedling as this can damage the delicate plant. It is usually quite sufficient to settle the compost around the roots by watering in, taking care to adjust appropriately if the seedling begins to topple over. Careful watering with a fine rose should help to avoid this.

When young seedlings are being germinated, it is quite possible that disease can set in. If this becomes apparent, take immediate action by removing any diseased areas and treating the remainder with an appropriate fungicide.

CUTTINGS

*P*ropagating plants from cuttings offers the benefit of reproducing accurately the plant from which the cutting was taken. The cutting itself may vary, being a stem cutting, tip cutting, heel cutting, leaf cutting or offset. The removal of any type depends upon the plant and you may find that some can be obtained simply by a nimble pinching action of the thumb and finger while others require the use of a pair of secateurs or pruning shears.

Tip cuttings and stem cuttings are very similar and really

Long trailing stems of Ficus pumila provide ideal material for propagation.

Take care to keep cuttings the right way round.

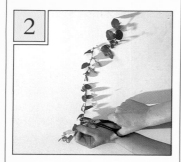

Cut long stems with vine scissors or secateurs.

Dibble cuttings into pot after dipping in hormone rooting powder.

only differ in that a stem cutting is usually simply a tip cutting without the growing tip, that is, it is part of the same stem but lower down. However, other types of stem cutting are to be found in plants such as dieffenbachia and dracaena where the actual stem of the plant may form the propagation material. Tip cuttings should be prepared (prior to placing in the appropriate medium) by cutting cleanly below a node (leaf joint) and stem cuttings by cutting just above a node. Cutting back too close to the upper node may damage the potential new shoot, while leaving too long a length of stem may result in die-back. The lower leaf or leaves may also need to be cleanly removed so that when the cutting is inserted no leaf tissue is buried or, for that matter, even allowed to be in contact with the surface of the compost. Failure to do this will almost certainly result in leaf rotting, which could destroy the cutting.

Stem cuttings of the larger type should be prepared similarly, whether they are inserted or laid on the compost. In all cases wounds must be clean to enable them to heal efficiently. Jagged cut areas or bruised tissue is an open invitation to disease and subsequent loss.

Heel cuttings are actually prepared by gently pulling off a branch or shoot of a plant complete with a piece of tissue from the main stem of the plant on which it was growing. When taking heel cuttings, try to minimize the amount of damage caused to the main stem by any bark being torn off, other than that in the immediate area of the base of the cutting. Where necessary, strip lower leaves off the cutting prior to insertion.

Leaf cuttings may take the form of either part of the leaf or the entire leaf and may be propagated in various ways according to the variety of plant. However, take care to select healthy mature leaves that are not too old or damaged or diseased. Where leaves are to be cut or stems of leaves inserted, take care to use clean sharp cutting implements.

OFFSETS

*O*ffsets may be produced in various ways from the base of the parent, or even from the top, as in the case of the earth star or cryptanthus. Where offsets can be cleanly removed they can be 'directly stuck' or potted if they are removed with roots attached. The key to propagating successfully from offsets is never to remove material that is too young, but to select the offset at the right stage and treat it in the appropriate manner.

BASIC TECHNIQUES OF PROPAGATION

Offset propagation of Spathiphyllum Wallisii: see page 118.

Air layering Ficus Robusta: see page 74.

LAYERING

Some varieties of plant such as cholorophytum may be propagated by layering. In its simplest of forms this involves placing an offshoot of the parent on or in a separate pot of compost while still attached to the parent. This allows the new plant gradually to develop its own root system while still being supplied with nutrients by its parent, until such time as the young plant is capable of growing on its own, at which time the connecting stem may be cleanly severed.

Another form of layering is air layering, where a plant is encouraged to propagate above soil level, as in the case of the rubber plant, *Ficus robusta*. Once the plant above the 'layered' area has developed a root system capable of supporting it, the new plant may be cut from the main plant just below the area and then potted up on its own.

ROOTING IN WATER

Apart from striking cuttings in a conventional seed and cutting compost, it is possible to root cuttings by other means.

A popular method is to root certain plants in water. This can be quite fun, but sometimes produces a more brittle and less fibrous root system so that particular care is required when the cuttings are potted up.

ROOTING GEL

Alternatively, a method gaining widespread interest is the use of a rooting gel. This clear, rubbery substance works in many ways like water, but propagates a much wider range of plants more successfully. The technique is simplicity itself. Once the cuttings are taken, holes are dibbled through the foil membrane in the small plastic container and the cuttings inserted into the gel. Rooting can be observed through the clear plastic container and cuttings removed and potted up when a sufficient root system has developed.

Fuchsia.

Columnea.

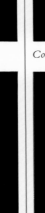

Coleus.

Hedera.

HORMONE ROOTING POWDER

Apart from when using rooting gel or water, you may wish to use a hormone rooting powder for greater success with many types of cutting. This works by encouraging the piece of plant to produce roots more readily. In certain cases formulations also include a fungicide to reduce losses from rotting off.

PESTS AND DISEASES

*I*t is absolutely fundamental to ensure that any material used for propagation purposes is free from pests and diseases. Care taken to ensure that plants are pest- and disease-free will certainly improve the success rate, or at the very least reduce the scale of the problem.

Although pests can be a real nuisance, the biggest problem that you are likely to face is the control of fungal diseases. The use of a hormone rooting powder with a fungicide incorporated may help to reduce some fungal problems, but will not help when a plant is infected with a disease.

DISEASES

*I*f a plant is infected with a disease such as mildew or rust it is better to delay propagation for several weeks to try to get the disease under control using fungicides based on copper, sulphur or zinc. Unfortunately, while attempting to gain control of the disease, it is quite likely that the key period to propagate the plant may be missed. It is, therefore, much better to treat plants that are known to suffer from particular fungal problems regularly to prevent the disease from gaining a hold in the first place.

Plants that are suffering from root or stem rots are not worth propagating from as the plant tissue is unlikely to be healthy enough to 'take' effectively. It is also possible that the disease organism may be transferred with the cutting.

Diseases such as 'grey mould fungus' or *botrytis* tend to be nuisance fungi that live on decaying tissue such as dead leaves or flowers. However, under the right conditions they can become more than a nuisance and can infect and kill living plant tissue. The use of systemic fungicides, such

Botrytis or grey mould fungus is a common problem during propagation, *as on the cactus (left) and aglaonema (right).*

as benomyl, which are translocated through the plant will not only control the organism but will also help to prevent further infection.

It is never sensible to propagate from plants that are suffering from fungal diseases. Sometimes the disease can dramatically increase in severity during propagation, especially if the cutting is enclosed within a polythene bag or some other sort of protected environment. Where problems are suspected it may be worth treating the plant with a preventative spray or drench (watering with spray strength solution) of a broad-spectrum systemic fungicide. This may help to prevent the development of quite a range of fungal problems.

Pests can also become a nuisance during the propagation period. As with fungal diseases, it is better to prepare the plant beforehand to ensure that it is clean before propagating than to find later that the plant is plagued by a pest. Treating a plant during the propagation period is generally quite unwise as the plant is very vulnerable to damage during this period.

Sooty mould, an indication of the presence of aphids and other pests.

Mildew can be transferred easily on propagation material.

Aphids or greenfly commonly attack the young leaf tissue.

Scale insects look like tiny blisters on the plant and may be found feeding on the stems and close to the leaf veins.

Mealy bugs are often seen as the characteristic white woolly patches found in the leaf axils and on leaf undersides.

Red spider mites are almost invisible to the naked eye, although the adults may be seen with the aid of a magnifying lens on the leaf undersides.

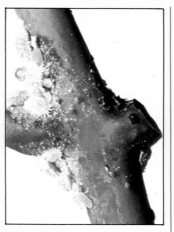

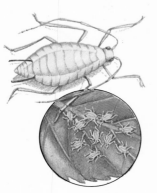

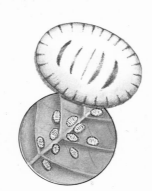

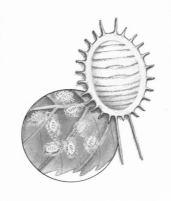

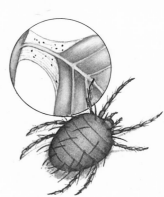

PESTS

*P*ests such as aphids (greenfly, blackfly) will build up to a major infestation within a very short period, especially during the spring and summer where it will be found to be most active on young growth. Spray with pirmicarb, permethrin or pyrethrum to effect a rapid 'knock-down' of the insect.

The scale insect is a relatively slow-moving pest that tends to stay within a particular area. It is, however, difficult to eradicate and care should be taken to control it effectively before propagating. Watch out for these 'blister-like' insects attached to the stems or leaves of plants and spray regularly with a systemic insecticide such as dimethoate, or contact insecticides such as malathion or permethrin.

Mealy bugs tend to live in the gap between the leaf stalk and the main stem of plants as well as in little crevices or areas close to the plant's main veins where they can hide. Looking like little pieces of cotton wool or small white powder-covered woodlice, they are similar to scale insects in that they do not move about much, but are easily spread

during propagation. Use similar insecticides to control them such as dimethoate, malathion or permethrin.

Whitefly are actually small moths that raise their young on the undersides of leaves. They tend to be more of a nuisance than anything else, but should be controlled before they get out of hand and a high population builds up. Regular spraying with permethrin or pyrethrum will effectively control them.

A pest that can be really difficult to spot, let alone control, is the red spider mite, a tiny mite that is actually straw-coloured rather than red in hue. It lives on the undersides of leaves, chewing the tissue and leaving it looking dull, speckled with large areas of necrosis. Webbing on the top growth is a sign of a very advanced infestation and spraying should have been started well before this to try to gain control. Spraying with dimethoate, malathion pirimiphos-methyl or rotenone will help to control the pest, providing it is done regularly and thoroughly, taking care to wet all leaf undersides.

Other pests such as fungus gnats, caterpillars and thrips may be occasional problems, but can be kept under control using permethrin or pyrethrum.

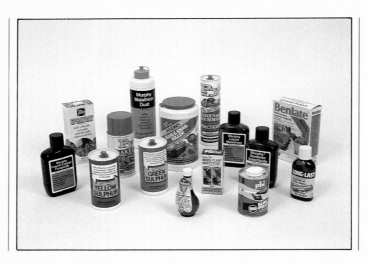

A selection of some of the many pesticides available.

Where possible, try to use low toxicity chemicals and, if possible, chemicals with a short life, such as pyrethrum, to the benefit of the environment.

Take particular care to use chemicals wisely and safely. Keep them well away from wildlife, pets, children, waterways and food, and dispose of them safely. NEVER FORGET THAT THESE SUBSTANCES ARE POISONS. Always use them according to the manufacturer's recommendations at the rates of use set out, taking

particular care to follow safety precautions regarding the handling, use and storage of the material.

Some chemicals can damage plants and may scorch them particularly if applied in full sun when the compost is on the dry side. Take care to ensure that the material that you have selected to use is safe to apply to the plant. Again, take full note of the manufacturer's recommendations and if in doubt, consult them for advice.

❚ AFTER-CARE ❚

*O*nce a plant has been successfully propagated, it is all too easy to increase the possibility of failure by reducing the amount of care provided. A newly propagated plant is relatively delicate and requires some degree of special care to ensure that the plant grows healthily and with vigour.

WATERING

*I*t is very easy to over-water a new plant and to damage or destroy a newly developing root system. It is essential not to keep the compost too wet. Indeed, for many subjects it is actually better to allow the compost almost to dry out to avoid any root loss that can occur if the compost is kept permanently wet.

Plastic pots tend to give a false reading when viewed at a casual glance. Although the surface of the compost may appear dry, the main volume could still be wet because a plastic pot conserves water and the compost tends only really to show signs of drying out on top. Check the level of moisture by gently probing the compost with a finger, watering as required.

It is equally important not to allow the compost to dry

right out; striking the right balance will help to ensure that the young roots are not damaged and that they will continue to develop to form a strong, well-balanced root system.

FEEDING

*A*s plants grow it is essential to attend to their nutritional needs, especially as some plants may well have been 'direct stuck' (that is rooted and grown on) in seed and cutting compost, which has an inherently low nutrient level.

Newly propagated plants are probably best fed with a dilute liquid houseplant fertilizer applied every two weeks or so during the active growing season of late spring to early autumn. Initially it should be used at about quarter rate, increasing it to half rate and, finally, as the plant develops a strong root system, to the normal rate recommended by the fertilizer manufacturer.

Never apply a liquid fertilizer to a dry plant as this can seriously damage or kill the plant. Moisten the compost first with plain water and then apply a liquid fertilizer. Do not apply the fertilizer at too fast a rate during the growing season as this can have equally serious effects.

Once the framework of a flowering plant has been built up with a conventional houseplant fertilizer, it may be worth using a special flowering-plant fertilizer to help produce more stocky, less lush, growth with the potential to produce a good display of flowers. A tomato fertilizer which is high in potassium may be used, but dilute it at about one-third of the rate recommended for tomatoes.

WEANING

*O*nce the plant has emerged from its carefully controlled environment and has possibly been removed from the protection of a plastic cover it will need to be weaned and 'hardened off'. This basically means that the plant has to begin to adapt to a greater variance in temperature, albeit within the range that it will happily tolerate. It may, therefore, be advisable not to suddenly change the environment, but to make the change gradually to help the plant harden off slowly. If you have been using a bag, start by removing it for a few hours a day, then increase the period accordingly.

Eventually the new plant will need to be grown on in its new position. Take care to provide it with the correct temperature and in particular try to avoid draughts in the first few weeks.

Plants that have been raised under cover are usually less hardy and may be particularly susceptible to sun scorch and dry atmospheric conditions. To reduce the problems caused by these factors, take care over the positioning as regards sunlight, and improve the level of humidity around plants that especially need it. This may be achieved by regularly misting with tepid water and, to some degree, by grouping plants together or standing them on dampened pebbles.

During the entire weaning process arrange the local environment around the plant so as to avoid draughts, temperature fluctuations, excessive heat, cold or light. Aim for moderation in all circumstances.

GROWING ON

*A*s the plants actively grow and develop, be prepared to carry out the normal procedures that one should with any healthy plant. Actively growing plants may well need to be repotted even during the season in which the plant was propagated, provided its growth rate warrants it.

Ensure that the minimum of disturbance is caused to the root system to avoid any check to growth. A useful way to repot is to knock the plant out of its pot and to use the old pot as a mould. Place the old pot inside the new and infill with compost between the two. Then remove the old pot, thus leaving a mould for the plant to be placed in with the minimum of disturbance.

Healthily growing plants will also need to be trimmed where appropriate on a support frame. This should be used sooner rather than later for climbing plants, to ensure that the best-shaped plant is created right from the beginning, rather than as an afterthought.

It is equally important to trim plants to maintain the correct habit of growth from an early enough stage. Do not allow a cutting to grow out of control to become a leggy, useless specimen, when with care and pinching or trimming at the right stage it could form a well-shaped, bushy plant.

*I*ncluded in the following techniques are indica-
tions as to which plants can be propagated fairly
easily, and those which require greater attention.
Browallia seedlings, for example, will practically leap out at
you, while only a small percentage of *Araucaria* seeds sown
will germinate. Although with some plants – such as
Fatshedera lizei – there are short cuts, patience is a virtue.
Some plants have their own peculiarities, as indicated: thus
Gardenia jasminoides will not thrive in compost with a high
pH level, and *Howea forsteriana* needs a high temperature.
In general, attentive control of the environment around the
newly propagated material is the key to success.

ABUTILON MEGAPOTAMICUM

*T*he abutilon can be easily propagated from mid-spring to early summer.

Select tip cuttings of 3–4in (7.5–10cm) and dip in hormone rooting powder in a seed and cutting compost, using a 3½in (9cm) pot and one cutting per pot or, alternatively, a 5½in (15cm) half-pot or pan into which three cuttings may be dibbled.

As the abutilon has a thin leaf and loses water easily, it is necessary either regularly to mist the foliage lightly or, alternatively, cover the cuttings with a clear plastic bag. The cuttings should be kept in an indirectly lit situation at a temperature of approximately 65–70°F (18–21°C) and the compost kept evenly moist.

After about a month rooting should start to develop and, when established sufficiently to dispense with the mist or plastic cover, the plant may be weaned, then gently removed from the pot and potted on in a potting compost in a 5½in (13cm) pot.

Abutilon may also be propagated from seed, although this is not recommended, particularly with variegated varieties, as these rarely come true.

ACALYPHA HISPIDA

*A*calypha are tall and can become rather untidy after a while. In order to reproduce a more compact and balanced plant it will be necessary to re-propagate.

In early to late spring, well prior to the plant producing flowers, take 3–4in (7.5–10cm) tip cuttings. Alternatively, gently break off newly produced side-shoots with a heel (the base of the side-shoot attached to the main stem) of a similar length.

These should then be dipped in hormone rooting powder and inserted one per pot in 3½in (9cm) pots in a well-lit, but sheltered, position away from direct sunlight.

The cuttings should be covered with a clear plastic bag to conserve water in the leaf tissue and avoid excessive transpiration. The seed and cutting compost should be evenly moist at the start of the operation and may not need to be remoistened while the cutting is rooting.

Maintain the cuttings at a temperature of 68–72°F (20–22°C). When they have started to grow after rooting, they can be potted on in a conventional potting compost in a 4¼in (11cm) or 5in (13cm) pot.

A

ACHIMENES GRANDIFLORA

*A*chimenes can be propagated easily by two methods that are usually successful in the home.

In late spring to early summer the plant can be propagated from 3–3½in (7.5–9cm) tip cuttings dipped into hormone rooting powder and then dibbled into the same peat-based potting compost that the mother plant grows in. Cuttings can either be dibbled in three to a 3½in (9cm) pot or five to a 5in (13cm) pot.

Alternatively, the plant may also be propagated at a similar time by removing the mother plant from its pot and teasing or gently cutting off pieces of the root or rhizome. These can then be potted up using similar pots and compost to that used for cuttings.

In both cases the plant should be kept at around 68°F (20°C) and kept evenly moist in a well-lit position out of direct sunlight.

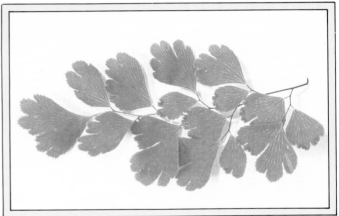

ADIANTUM CAPILLUS-VENERIS

*A*diantum can most easily be propagated by splitting up the mother plant almost at any time of the year, although greater success will probably be achieved during the growing season.

The plant should be removed from its pot, ensuring that the compost is evenly moistened first, to ease the teasing off of pieces of the root or rhizome for propagation. Using a sharp knife, cut off and remove pieces with fronds growing on them.

Larger plants can obviously be created by teasing and, if necessary, cutting apart larger pieces or clumps.

The individual pieces may then be potted up in 3½in (9cm) pots, using a peat-based potting compost. Take care to keep the plants in a position away from direct sunlight at a temperature of about 65–68°F (18–20°C). It is also important to ensure that a high level of humidity is maintained after this activity and that the compost is kept evenly moist, but not over-watered; otherwise failure may well result.

AECHMEA FASCIATA

When the mature aechmea or urn plant has flowered, it will produce offsets around the base of the mother plant. In normal household conditions the aechmea will produce from one to three offsets and sometimes more under exceptional circumstances.

It is important to wait until the offsets are approximately one-half to two-thirds of the size of the mother plant when they may be removed and potted up singly. In order to do this, the compost should be evenly moistened. Then, using a sharp knife, carefully separate the offset from its mother, taking care to 'feel' the way between the plants to avoid damaging the base of the plants. Patience at this stage will be rewarded.

Once separated, the plants may then be potted in a suitable bromeliad compost or peat-based seed and cutting compost in a 4¼in (11cm) pot and kept at about 68°F (20°C).

Do not keep the compost too moist, but try to maintain a regime where moisture can just be detected, as this helps to ensure faster rooting and establishment. Also keep the plant out of direct sunlight until you are certain that it has survived the move. Spring or early summer is the best time for this activity.

Finally, it is important to remember that after flowering the mother plant eventually dies; so do not be tempted to give away all the offspring!

AESCHYNANTHUS BOSCHANUS

*Y*ou should be able to propagate aeschynanthus throughout the year, although the plant will obviously root more rapidly in the spring and summer.

The plant can be propagated readily by removing sections of the long trailing stems and cutting them into 3–4in (7.5–10cm) pieces to form tip or stem cuttings. After dipping into hormone rooting powder dibble the cuttings three to a 3½in (9cm) pot or five to a 5½in (14cm) half-pot or pan, using a seed and cutting compost that is peat based. Try to ensure that tip cuttings and stem cuttings are potted separately as this helps to provide more balanced plants. Also take care to ensure that the compost is not too moist.

Cover the plants with clear plastic bags to improve the level of humidity and maintain a temperature of around 70°F (21°C).

Once the plants have satisfactorily rooted, after about six to eight weeks, the bag can be removed and the plants grown on in a well-lit position out of direct sunlight.

Aeschynanthus may also be propagated singly in a similar way using 2½in (6cm) pots, before being potted up with other rooted cuttings into a larger pot. This method may be useful if rotting occurs which can spread to other cuttings in the same pot.

AGAVE AMERICANA 'MARGINATA'

*T*he agave is not the sort of plant to keep in a house with children around, but it is certainly a test of acute dexterity for the enthusiast to propagate.

The fleshy succulent leaves are tough and leathery and are protected by fierce needle-sharp hooked barbs along the edges, with an extra long and equally sharp needle-point at the leaf tip.

Propagation requires the greatest care and skill to protect yourself rather than the plant. When the plant has produced offsets that measure about 4in (10cm) they can be separated from the mother plant and potted up on their own during the spring and summer.

Wear heavy protective gardening gloves, and protect your eyes with goggles. Use rolled newspaper to wrap around the plant to remove it from its pot, taking care to hold the plant away from you.

Then take a sharp knife and, by a process of teasing apart and separating and cutting, remove the offset and pot it up in cacti and succulent potting compost in a 4¼in (11cm) pot. Use a clay pot if possible.

The offset should then be kept with hardly any moisture in the compost to encourage rapid development of roots and grown at a temperature of around 65°F (18°C).

A magnificent specimen of Agave Americana growing outdoors; except in the mildest of climes, the plant needs to be taken indoors for the winter.

1

Remove plant from its pot.

2

Use thumbs to gently divide plant.

AGLAONEMA CRISPUM 'SILVER QUEEN'

*A*glaonema may be propagated in a number of ways. The most popular and the one that probably causes the least amount of damage to the plant is to separate sideshoots from the base of the plant.

In mid-spring to early summer remove the plant from its pot and remove side-shoots that have several leaves. Do not remove any that only have two leaves and, where possible, try to acquire some root, preferably attached to the shoot. A sharp knife may ease the process.

The shoot should then be potted in an open peat-based compost in a 3½in (9cm) pot and covered with a clear plastic bag to conserve moisture. Rooting will take several weeks, even up to a couple of months. Keep the plant at a temperature of 68–70°F (20–21°C) out of direct sunlight.

Apart from being raised from seed propagated at around 75°F (24°C) from late spring, aglaonema can also be propagated from sections of the stem. This technique is suitable for overgrown, untidy and leggy specimens that have outgrown their usefulness.

Stem sections measuring 1½–2in (4–5cm) can be pressed into the surface of the compost until about one-quarter to one-third of the stem is buried. Maintain a temperature of around 75°F (24°C) and keep the compost moist, potting up the plantlets when they are large enough to handle.

3

Separate into plantlets with more than two leaves.

4

Pot up shoot in open peat-based compost and cover with a clear plastic bag.

A

| ALLAMANDA CATHARTICA | ALOE VARIEGATA |

*A*llamanda may be propagated from tip cuttings. The time for this is mid-spring to early summer and the tips should measure approximately 3–4in (7.5–10cm).

Dip the base of the stem of each cutting into hormone rooting powder and then dibble into a 3½in (9cm) pot, one cutting per pot. The cutting should then be covered with a clear plastic bag and a temperature of 70–72°F (21–22°C) maintained until rooting has taken place, after about six to eight weeks.

Allamanda prefers a reasonably high light level. Nevertheless, try to avoid excessive direct sunlight.

Once rooted well, around three months, the young plant may then be potted up into a 5in (13cm) pot using a conventional potting compost. There is no need to continue using the plastic bag to cover the plant once rooting has developed, even prior to repotting.

*A*loe produces offsets fairly readily which offer by far the easiest means of propagation.

In late spring or early summer plants that have produced offsets should be removed from the pot. Offsets that have started to form their own defined rosettes should be gently teased away from the parent, taking care not to break the stem. Try to remove as much of the attached root with the offset.

Once the offset has been removed, pot it up singly in a 3½in (9cm) pot using a cacti and succulent compost. The plant should be kept in good light without too much direct sunlight until sufficiently rooted, about two to three months. Maintain a temperature of 65–68°F (18–20°C) and ensure that the compost is barely moist to encourage more rapid root development.

Although offsets are readily produced by aloe, do not be tempted to remove them when they are small; they do not tend to root as readily as larger offsets.

ANANAS COMOSUS VARIEGATUS

*T*he variegated pineapple may be propagated by two methods, using the rosette from the top of the fruit and the offsets that form around the base of the plant. The former is much more difficult, whereas offsets offer the best chance of success.

In order to root the rosette, carefully cut off the top of the fruit as well so that about ½in (1.5cm) is attached to the base of the rosette. Allow this to dry for a day or so out of direct sunlight and then dip it into hormone rooting powder and lightly press into a 4¼in (11cm) pot filled with seed and cutting compost, covering the plant and pot with a clear plastic bag.

Maintain a temperature of 75–80°F (24–27°C) until rooting has taken place; this can take up to two months or more.

When offsets are 4in (10cm) they may be carefully pared from the parent with a sharp knife and potted singly in a 3½–4¼in (9–11cm) pot filled with seed and cutting compost. Remember to dip the base of the offset in hormone rooting powder first.

Cover the plant and pot with a plastic bag and keep the compost barely moist at a temperature of around 75°F (24°C) to enable rooting to take place. Again, this may take up to two months.

As relatively high temperatures are required, propagation of ananas is best left until mid-spring to mid-summer when ambient temperatures should be higher. Avoid too much direct light during the initial stages of propagation.

A

ANTHURIUM ANDREANUM

Anthurium produces a mass of fleshy and relatively brittle roots which appear to push the plant out of its pot. With care the plant may be propagated by carefully teasing apart the clump of roots where separate plants can be seen.

It is important to ensure that the compost is moist and that you do not pull the clump apart haphazardly, but try to identify where there is active development of new growth as well as leaves. The best time to do this is from mid-spring to mid-summer when new plantlets tend to develop more freely.

Once separated, trim off any old, damaged or diseased roots and pot up in a 4¼–5in (11–13cm) pot, using a peaty potting compost into which sphagnum moss has been incorporated to produce an open compost. Do not bury the plantlets when planting, but try to keep them proud of the surface.

Keep the plantlets at a temperature of 75°F (24°C) with a high level of humidity, using a clear plastic bag cover or regular misting to enhance the environment.

Anthurium may also be propagated from seed germinated in a similar compost at the temperature used for propagating.

You may find *Anthurium scherzerianum* slightly easier to propagate as it has tougher, more leathery leaf tissue that loses water less readily. However, varieties such as *Anthurium crystallinum* require a far higher level of humidity and may be much more difficult to propagate.

APHELANDRA SQUARROSA 'LOUISAE'

Aphelandra may be propagated from stem or tip cuttings in mid-spring to early summer for best success, although it is possible to root cuttings through the summer.

Tip cuttings measuring up to 3in (7.5cm), or stem cuttings consisting of a pair of leaves with about 2in (5cm) of stem below the leaves, may be used.

Dip the base of the cutting in hormone rooting powder and insert one per pot into a 4¼in (11cm) pot in a peat-based potting compost. If the leaves of the stem cutting are too large, trim off the tips with a sharp pair of scissors.

Cover the cutting and pot with a clear plastic bag and keep out of direct sunlight at a temperature of around 70–75°F (21–24°C) for up to about six weeks while the cutting is developing a root system.

Once rooted, remove the bag and grow the plant on, keeping the compost moist and potting on as required.

Tip cuttings tend to produce a more balanced plant with a single stem, whereas stem cuttings can sometimes produce a plant that may look a little out of balance if one side-shoot develops before the other.

ARAUCARIA HETEROPHYLLA

*T*he araucaria is not an easy plant to propagate, but with perseverance the enthusiast will obtain success.

This plant is probably best propagated from seed sown from mid-spring to early summer at a temperature of around 68°F (20°C). Seed can be thinly sown either in trays or shallow pans or half-pots (5½in [14cm] are the ideal size), using a seed and cutting compost.

Try to increase the humidity level by covering the container with either a sheet of clear plastic or glass, but avoid an excessive build-up of moisture by removing it occasionally. Alternatively, leave a small space for ventilation.

When the seed has germinated – and you may only achieve a 10 per cent germination rate – leave the seedlings until they are about 2–3in (5–7.5cm) tall, growing them in a well-lit position to avoid etiolation of the stems.

Gently prick out and pot up the seedlings in 3½in (9cm) pots of a peat-based potting compost.

ASPARAGUS SETACEUS

*A*asparagus may be propagated from seed sown in the spring at a temperature of around 70°F (21°C) in a seed and cutting compost, although you will find this method is rather slow. Even when seedlings have germinated, their rate of growth is slow and you will have to wait some months before you have a plant of a reasonable size.

A better method of raising a plant more rapidly is to separate the mother plant in mid-spring to early summer.

Moisten the compost and remove the plant from its pot. Tease the plant's roots apart, using a sharp knife, and separate the clump into manageable pieces that can be potted up into 3½in (9cm) pots using a peat-based potting compost.

Be sure to keep the compost evenly moist and grow the plants on in a reasonably well-lit position well out of direct sunlight.

ASPIDISTRA ELATIOR

spidistra is not by any means the fastest growing of houseplants although it is long lived. You need to bear this in mind when propagating the plant to gain the best effect from the new plants.

Mid-spring to early summer is an ideal time for separating the fairly massive rhizomes. Tease pieces of plant, with two or more leaves on each piece, away from the parent. Use a sharp knife to sever the rhizome where necessary.

The individual pieces can then be potted up singly in a 3½–4¼in (9–11cm) pot using a peat-based potting compost. Alternatively, for a better effect, pot two or three small plants together in a pot.

Maintain a temperature of 65–68°F (18–20°C) and keep the compost barely moist. This is particularly important for the first few weeks after separation to promote more rapid root production.

Tap spores onto a sheet of paper.

Sprinkle spores thinly onto the surface of the moistened compost.

ASPLENIUM NIDUS

The asplenium, like most ferns, can be difficult to propagate, but the keen enthusiast will find it well worth attempting.

Spores are produced from gill-like protrusions on the underside of mature fronds. These may be collected by lightly tapping the fronds over a sheet of white paper. The brown spores may be seen as a fine dust-like powder on the paper.

Prior to sowing the spores, fill a seed tray, pan or half-pot with a peat-based seed and cutting compost and lightly moisten.

Sow the spores very thinly on the surface of the compost and cover with a piece of newspaper over the top to keep out excessive light.

Aim to maintain a temperature of around 70°F (21°C) until the spores germinate. If they germinate too thickly prick them out to give them more space, treating them in much the same way as germinating the spores of *Platycerium bifurcatum*. However, this problem is unlikely to occur as germination is usually slow.

When the young plants are large enough to handle, approximately ½–1in (1–2.5cm), pot them up singly in a 2½in (6cm) pot using a peat-based compost, and then later into a 3½–4¼in (9–11cm) pot.

A

AUCUBA JAPONICA VARIEGATA

*A*ucuba may be propagated from mid-spring to early summer, taking 4–5in (10–12.5cm) tip cuttings.

The cuttings should be dipped in hormone rooting powder and then inserted one per pot in 3½in (9cm) pots of seed and cutting compost.

Although the foliage is relatively waxy and conserves water moderately well, it is advisable to cover each cutting with a clear plastic bag. This will help to reduce transpiration and promote more rapid rooting.

After being kept at about 68°F (20°C) for a few weeks, the cutting should have rooted sufficiently to be removed from the bag and potted up in a 4¼–5in (11–13cm) pot using a potting compost.

The aucuba likes a high level of light, but, during propagation try to avoid exposure to direct sunlight.

Remove 4–5in (10–12.5cm) tip cuttings.

Hold cutting gently by stem.

Remove lower leaves.

Dip base of cutting in hormone rooting powder.

Insert cutting in 3½in (9cm) pot of seed and cutting compost.

Insert two sticks, one on each side of pot.

Cover cutting with clear plastic bag.

Secure bag with elastic band.

AZALEA INDICA

*T*he Indian azalea is not that easy to propagate successfully, but is worth attempting from late spring to early summer.

Dip 2–3in (5–7.5cm) tip cuttings into hormone rooting powder and insert one per 2¼–3½in (6–9cm) pot of a peat-based seed and cutting compost or low-lime compost with a lower pH (higher level of acidity).

Cover each cutting with a clear polythene bag or, alternatively, mist regularly to reduce water loss from the foliage. Maintain a temperature of 68–70°F (20–21°C), keeping the cuttings in light shade.

Rooting may take up to three months, after which the rooted cuttings may be potted up in a 3½–4¼in (9–11cm) pot of a peat-based low-lime compost, watering where possible with rainwater to avoid the damaging effects of calcium deposits in tap water.

Remove 2–3in (5–7.5cm) tip cuttings.

Carefully remove lower leaves.

After dipping base of cutting in hormone rooting powder, insert one per 2¼–3½in (6–9cm) pot.

Cover cutting with clear plastic bag.

B

BEGONIA ELATIOR

Begonia elatior may be propagated from tip cuttings with a small section of stem attached.

The tip cutting may be prepared by using a sharp knife to cut cleanly to remove a tip cutting of 3–4in (7.5–10cm). The cut surface should then be lightly dusted with hormone rooting powder and dibbled one per pot into a 2¼–3½in (6–9cm) pot of seed and cutting compost. Although not really necessary, support may be supplied by a small stick to keep the leaf secure in its pot while rooting takes place.

A clear plastic bag placed over each cutting will help to increase humidity and more rapid rooting.

Keeping the cutting at 68–70°F (20–21°C), rooting should take place within about a month, after which the cutting will grow to produce plantlets.

If you wish to build up your stock the plantlets may be separated once large enough to handle and potted up singly in a 3½in (9cm) pot, using a peat-based potting compost and grown on before being potted on in the final pot.

Alternatively, the clump of plantlets may be potted up into a 4¼in (11cm) pot, although this may tend to lead to a more crowded plant of varied habit.

Cuttings may be taken in the spring and summer, and plants propagated early on in the season will flower in the same year.

1

Use sharp knife to remove 3–4in (7.5–10cm) tip cutting.

2

Hold stem gently and dip in hormone rooting powder.

3

Insert cutting, one per 2¼–3½in (6–9cm) pot.

4

Cover cutting with clear plastic bag.

BEGONIA REX

*T*he *Begonia rex* may be propagated by a most un-usual procedure using postage stamp pieces of leaf to raise new plants.

During spring and summer the plant may be propagated by selecting a mature leaf, taking care not to use a leaf that is too old. Using a very sharp knife, cut the leaf into roughly postage stamp sized pieces, taking care not to bruise the tissue or cut any fingers.

The pieces should then be gently held and the cut surfaces across the main veins lightly dipped into hormone rooting powder. The pieces may then be laid on the surface of a seed tray or 5½in (14cm) pan filled with seed and cutting compost or gently pressed into the surface, ensuring that the cut vein is in close contact with the compost.

Cover the leaf pieces with clear plastic, glass or poly-thene and maintain a temperature of around 70°F (21°C) until rooting has taken place and small plantlets have formed. Regularly inspect the leaf squares and rapidly discard any that are showing signs of rotting off. If this occurs you may need to use a fungicide to avoid further losses.

Once growth occurs the cover may be removed and the plantlets grown on until about 1½in (2.5cm) tall. They may then be gently separated and potted up singly in a 3½in (9cm) pot of a peat-based potting compost.

Remove mature leaf with sharp knife.

Carefully cut leaf into postage stamp sized pieces.

Having cut leaf, lightly dust undersides of leaf pieces with hormone rooting powder.

Lay leaf pieces gently on surface of compost.

B

BELOPERONE GUTTATA

*B*eloperone may be successfully propagated by either tip or stem cuttings from mid-spring to early summer when conditions favour more effective rooting.

Remove tip cuttings measuring up to 3in (7.5cm) or stem cuttings of about 2in (5cm), using a sharp knife or scissors, and dip each cutting into hormone rooting powder. Dibble each cutting into a pot, ensuring that tip cuttings and stem cuttings are kept together if you wish to produce a bushy plant, unlike the more 'leggy' specimen pictured above.

Dibble three cuttings to a 3½in (9cm) pot and five cuttings to a 4¼in (11cm) pot, using a seed and cutting compost. Cover the cuttings with a plastic bag and maintain a temperature of around 68–70°F (20–21°C) until rooting has taken place, for up to a couple of months.

Keep the cuttings in good light, but out of direct sunlight to avoid scorch.

As soon as the cuttings have rooted, remove the plastic cover and if the cuttings have started actively to grow, commence feeding.

Beloperone can grow to be extremely straggly and regular pruning will be required after propagation to train the plant accordingly. Commercially grown beloperone are treated with a chemical growth retardant to produce a more compact habit of growth.

Failure to remove the bag cover may result in the new growth becoming etiolated, which will require early trimming to form a better-shaped plant.

B

BOUGAINVILLEA GLABRA

*A*lthough the bougainvillea is quite difficult to propagate in the home, it is certainly worth the effort. Success really requires a heated propagation unit to enable rooting to take place.

Tip or stem cuttings of bougainvillea may be taken of new growth from mid-spring to early summer, which may mean delaying the activity in the event of a poor or late spring to enable the mother plant to generate suitable material for propagation.

Cuttings measuring 4–6in (10–15cm) should be taken using a sharp knife or a pair of secateurs or pruning shears. Each cutting should then be dipped into hormone rooting powder before being dibbled into a 3½in (9cm) pot of seed and cutting compost, one cutting per pot.

The cutting should then be covered with a clear plastic bag and kept at a temperature of around 75°F (24°C) for anything up to two months, keeping the cutting in a well-lit, but not sunny, position to avoid scorch.

Once rooting has taken place, remove the polythene bag and pot the plant into a 5in (13cm) pot using a peat-based potting compost.

Due to the vigorous nature of bougainvillea when cultivated under correct conditions, it is important to train the plant onto a wire hoop or other support framework as soon as it starts to break into fresh growth. An untidy, messy plant may result in a very short space of time if this procedure is not followed.

BROWALLIA SPECIOSA

The brightly hued browallia may be propagated relatively easily from seed. Provided the seed is sown early enough in the gardening year it is possible to grow and flower the plant in the same year, with flowers appearing in late summer or early autumn, and lasting for several weeks.

Seed should be sown from early to mid-spring in either seed trays or 5½in (14cm) half-pots or pans filled with a seed and cutting compost.

Do not sow the seed thickly, otherwise pricking out will prove to be a difficult exercise which may result in damage to the young seedlings. Keep the compost moist and cover the container with clear plastic, glass or a plastic bag, taking care to ventilate occasionally to avoid excessive moisture build-up which could lead to damping off. Having kept the seed at about 65–68°F (18–20°C) in reasonable light, but out of direct sunlight, remove the cover as soon as germination has taken place.

When the seedlings are 1in (2.5cm) tall, gently prick them out and pot them up in a 3½in (9cm) pot of potting compost. It may be beneficial to cover the pricked-out seedlings for early sowings of the plant.

Once the seedlings have grown and filled the 3½in (9cm) pot, they may then be potted up a size or two to 4¼ or 5in (11 or 13cm) pots to produce the mature plant.

BRUNFELSIA CALYCINA MACRANTHA

*B*runfelsia may be propagated from either tip cuttings of the new season's growth produced in the spring or from the previous year's semi-hardwood growth.

Tip cuttings measuring about 4in (10cm) of the new season's growth should be removed in the spring using a sharp knife. The cutting should then be dipped into hormone rooting powder before being inserted in a 3½in (9cm) pot filled with seed and cutting compost, and covered with a clear plastic bag. Keeping the cutting at a temperature of 68–70°F (20–21°C) in a well-lit position out of direct sunlight, rooting should take place within a period of between one to two months.

Alternatively, prepare semi-hardwood cuttings of about 4in (10cm) and treat in the same manner until rooting has taken place.

When cuttings produced by either technique have sufficiently rooted and may be safely removed from the protection of the bag, they should be left in the pot and grown on before being potted on.

Regular feeding of the plant will encourage the plant to produce a healthy framework of foliage. After a further period of between three and four months the plant may then be potted up into a 5–7in (13–18cm) pot, using a peat-based potting compost.

CALADIUM 'CANDIDUM'

*T*he caladium grows from a tuber that lies dormant over winter after the active growing period during the spring and summer.

Prior to propagating the plant it is important to ensure that the tuber is stored and rested correctly over the winter period. Once the leaves have died back, the tuber should be stored almost dry at a temperature of around 60°F (16°C), care being taken to ensure that it is not infected with a fungal rot during this period.

In early spring, prior to starting the plant into growth, gently lift the tuber; young tubers should be found growing next to the mother plant. These may be carefully removed from the mother plant and potted up separately in a 3½–4¼in (9–11cm) pot, depending on the size of the tuber. An application of a broad-spectrum fungicide such as benomyl may be useful in preventing any rotting that could occur.

The tuber should be planted just below the surface of the peat-based potting compost which should be kept evenly moist and at a temperature of around 75°F (24°C).

Once the tuber has started to grow and produce leaves, the temperature may be reduced to around 68°F (20°C), but take particular care to ensure that the plant is not exposed to any draughts or the foliage will collapse.

CALATHEA MAKOYANA

$\mathcal{C}$alathea may be propagated simply by carefully dividing a well-formed clump of foliage, providing care is taken not to damage the plant in the procedure.

In mid-spring to early summer, when the plant is probably more capable of sustaining some disturbance, moisten the compost and remove the plant from its pot.

Using a process of gently teasing apart the clump to identify pieces that may be removed and propagated, with a sharp knife to clearly separate the pieces, remove sections with a few leaves which have roots attached.

Having carefully trimmed off any dead or damaged tissue, pot the individual pieces one per pot into a 3½in (9cm) pot of a peat-based potting compost. Alternatively, small clumps may be planted together for a fuller effect.

Either way, once potted up, the plant should be covered with a clear plastic gag to reduce transpiration and dehydration, and kept out of direct light. When the plant has rooted, in about six to eight weeks, the bag may be removed and the plant grown on as normal. If any leaf damage or rotting is noticed during the period under the polythene bag, which quite often occurs with thin-leaved calathea, remove the bag and trim off the affected tissue before any infection can spread. Try to maintain a temperature of around 68°F (20°C) at all times during the procedure.

Moisten compost and carefully remove plant from pot.

Gently tease apart clump.

Separate piece from main clump.

Pot into 3½in (9cm) pot of peat-based potting compost.

Gently firm compost to secure.

Cover plant with clear plastic bag.

CALCEOLARIA HERBEOHYBRIDA

*A*lthough calceolaria has a relatively short life as a flowering houseplant, it is worth propagating and growing for its range of brightly hued flowers, although you have to be patient to allow the plant to reach maturity.

Seed should be thinly sown in either seed trays, shallow pans or 5½in (14cm) half-pots or pans filled with seed and cutting compost. The seed should be sown from late spring to mid-summer and kept at a temperature of about 65–68°F (18–20°C). When the seed has germinated it is important to ensure that the developing seedlings are grown on in good light, otherwise they will become leggy and top-heavy.

As soon as the young seedlings are large enough to handle, the compost should be adequately moistened and the seedlings gently pricked out. They should then be potted up into 3½in (9cm) pots of a peat-based potting compost and grown on in a well-lit situation through the summer.

Having been grown during the winter period at a temperature of around 50°F (10°C) the plants will flower the following spring.

B

CALLISTEMON CITRINUS

The bottle-brush plant may be propagated from late spring to early summer for best results. Some success may be experienced from cuttings taken through the summer, but this tends to become progressively less.

Cuttings, measuring 3–4in (7.5–10cm), may be obtained from tip cuttings produced in the current season and which should be removed with a sharp knife, secateurs or pruning shears. Alternatively, before the new shoots become too long and as soon as they reach a length of between 3–4in (7.5–10cm) they may be gently removed from the plant by hand. To do this, grasp the shoot and pull it downwards to break it off with a 'heel'. Whatever type of cutting is selected, take care to ensure that there is no evidence of flowers appearing.

The cutting should then be dipped into a hormone rooting powder and dibbled into a 3½in (9cm) pot of seed and cutting compost and covered with a clear polythene bag to reduce water loss.

Rooting may take up to two months at a temperature of around 70°F (21°C). Keep the cutting in a well-lit position, but out of direct sunlight.

The polythene bag may then be removed and the plant grown on until it has matured more and has produced a good root system, in around three to four months. The plant may then be potted up in a peat-based potting compost in a 5–7in (13–18cm) pot.

C

CAMPANULA ISOPHYLLA

Campanula may be propagated either by division of the mother plant or by taking tip cuttings from mid-spring to early summer.

Division of the plant may appear to be the easiest, but great care should be taken to minimize damage to the plant. Simply teasing the clump of the plant apart is not enough, as not only the roots, but also the delicate and brittle foliage, may be damaged more than is necessary.

To minimize the damage, moisten the compost and carefully tease and cut apart the clump into manageable pieces that can be potted up into a 4¼–5in (11–13cm) pot of a peat-based potting compost. The gentle teasing away of some of the old compost may help the new roots to root readily into the fresh compost, but do not be too vigorous with this activity.

Cuttings may also be taken during the spring as soon as new growth is produced. 2–3in (5–7.5cm) tip cuttings should be carefully removed from the plant with a sharp knife, a pair of scissors or, if you are precise, but gentle, it is possible to pinch off the cuttings. However, the stems are very delicate; they are easily crushed and damaged which may prevent them from rooting and probably cause them to rot off.

The cutting should be dipped into hormone rooting powder. Then, using a small stick, dibble a hole into seed and potting compost, gently insert the cutting and firm it very lightly. Where possible, handle the cutting by its leaves rather than by holding its stem.

Cuttings may be inserted three to a 3½in (9cm) pot or five to a 4¼–5in (11–13cm) pot. They should then be covered with a clear polythene bag and kept at a temperature of around 65–68°F (18–20°C) in moderate light until well rooted, which should take place within a month. After this the bag may be removed and the cuttings then allowed to 'harden off'.

Cuttings may then either be grown on in the propagation pot, taking care to feed regularly with a liquid fertilizer, or potted on using a peat-based potting compost.

C

CAREX MORROWII VARIEGATA

*T*his variegated grass is very easy to propagate. Propagation also becomes almost essential as the plant will grow to fill its pot, thereby requiring either potting on or thinning to maintain healthy growth.

Healthy vigorous clumps of the grass can be thinned from mid-spring to early summer to provide propagation material. Moisten the compost and then tease the plant into clumps up to about 2in (5cm) in size. It may be necessary to use a sharp knife to ease the separation, but do not try to produce too many clumps which are too small. These rarely grow as strongly and it is better to produce fewer, but better sized, clumps.

Each individual clump should be potted up in a 3½–4¼in (9–11cm) pot using a peat-based potting compost.

No further special treatment is required and the new plant will establish itself quite quickly. However, to improve the level of humidity to reduce the possibility of the tips and edges of the leaves dehydrating it may be useful to mist the leaves regularly with tepid water.

The plant is quite tolerant of temperature, but a temperature around 68°F (20°C) should help to promote more rapid establishment.

C

CEROPEGIA WOODII

This curious hanging plant has long trailing stems which grow curious tubers along their length.

From mid-spring through to early summer the plant may be propagated either from the tubers that are produced on the stems or from stem cuttings.

Fill a 3½in (9cm) pot with a cactus and succulent compost and sprinkle a little sharp sand on the surface. Place about three of the tubers on the sand and keep the compost barely moist. Excessive watering will almost certainly result in the tubers rotting which will be disappointing, especially as this can happen after several weeks of waiting.

Alternatively, dip 2–3in (5–7.5cm) stem cuttings into hormone rooting powder and dibble three per 3½in (9cm) pot of similar compost, taking equal care over watering.

Rooting may take up to and even longer than two months before active growth develops and even then great care should be taken to ensure that the compost is kept on the dry side.

Although mature plants enjoy high light intensities, when propagating try to provide a little protection from direct sunlight. A temperature of 65–70°F (18–21°C) is ideal for rooting.

C

CHAMAEDOREA ELEGANS

*T*he propagation of the chamaedorea or parlour palm is worthwhile if you can provide ideal conditions for the seed to germinate.

The seed of the plant needs to be sown in a peat-based seed and cutting compost in either a seed tray or shallow pot or pan. Ideally, whatever container the seed is sown in should be placed in a heated propagation unit, unless you can provide a temperature that remains fairly constant at around 70°F (21°C) or even up to 75°F (24°C). The percentage of seed that germinates successfully is relatively low in comparison to other types of seed germinated.

Chamaedorea seed is probably best sown from mid-spring to early summer and should be kept in light shade. Germination may take many weeks and can be rather patchy. Make a close check for any fungal rots which can affect the lower stems of the young seedlings and cause damping off.

Once the seedlings are about 2in (5cm) tall they should be gently teased out of the compost and potted up either singly, or for a more dense-looking plant, up to three plants in a 3½in (9cm) pot, taking particular care not to over-water and continuing to keep a watch for fungal problems.

C

CHLOROPHYTUM COMOSUM 'VITTATUM'

*C*hlorophytum really is a fun plant to propagate and offers the enthusiast various ways of increasing the stock.

The long trailing stems produced by the mother plant carry tiny tufts of leaves which grow to develop into small plantlets. In time these plantlets grow roots even before the plantlet is anywhere near soil to root and grow in.

For the best chance of success the plantlets can simply be rested or lightly pressed into the surface of the compost in a 3½in (9cm) pot of peat-based potting compost. In time, and when the plantlet is ready, it will produce roots while still taking nutrients from the mother plant. As the roots develop the connecting stem may be severed and the young plantlet grown on, on its own.

Alternatively, plantlets may either be rooted in water when they are about 3in (7.5cm), and beginning to develop root buds at the base, or propagated in compost.

If rooted in water the plantlet can be left in a clear jar with its base submerged in water until its roots have developed, after which it can be potted up carefully into a 3½in (9cm) pot of potting compost.

Plantlets rooted directly into a 3½in (9cm) pot of potting compost should first be dipped into a hormone rooting powder before being lightly dibbled into the compost.

Propagation by either method may be carried out throughout the spring and summer at an ideal temperature of 65–68°F (18–20°C) in a well-lit position, but out of direct sunlight.

Lightly press plantlet into compost surface, place paper-clip over stem.

Gently press paper-clip to secure plantlet.

Leave plantlet to root whilst still attached to parent.

When roots have developed, cut the connecting stem.

C

CISSUS ANTARCTICA

Cissus antarctica, as well as being one of the easiest houseplants to care for, can be readily propagated by a technique known as 'direct sticking', similar to the one used in commercial production.

From early spring to early summer and even through the late summer months, you may carefully remove tip cuttings measuring around 3–5in (7.5–12.5cm) using a sharp knife, scissors, secateurs or pruning shears. The cuttings should then be dipped into hormone rooting powder and then carefully dibbled directly into the pot in which the plant will be grown on. It may prove necessary to remove the lower leaves in order to achieve this.

As a guide, insert three to four cuttings in a 3½in (9cm) pot, four to five cuttings in a 4¼in (11cm) pot, or five to six cuttings in a 5in (13cm) pot, filling each pot with a peat-based potting compost.

Cover each pot with a clear plastic bag to conserve humidity and keep them at a temperature of around 65–68°F (18–20°C). The cuttings should be kept in moderate light away from the scorching effects of the direct sun's rays. Rooting should take place after a few weeks.

Take care to remove any rotting leaves before the infection spreads. Once the cuttings start into new growth, a useful sign that rooting has started, the plastic bag can be removed and the plant grown on as normal, feeding as necessary to promote healthy active growth.

Rhoicissus rhomboidea, in many ways a similar plant, may be propagated using the same technique.

Remove 3–5in (7.5–12.5cm) tip cuttings.

Dip base in hormone rooting powder and insert three to four per 3½in (9cm) pot.

Insert two canes, one on either side of the pot.

Cover with clear plastic bag.

CITRUS MITIS

The *Citrus mitis* or calamondin orange is probably the most popular variety of citrus grown as a houseplant due to its compact habit and ability to bear fruit at a relatively diminutive height.

Propagation is not easy due to the prolonged warm temperatures and environmental control necessary, but this is a rewarding plant to grow.

From cuttings the procedure is relatively straightforward from mid-spring to early summer when conditions are more opportune. Stem cuttings measuring 4–6in (10–15cm) should be removed with secateurs or pruning shears and dipped into hormone rooting powder before being dibbled one per pot into a 3½in (9cm) pot of seed and cutting compost. The cutting should then be covered with a clear plastic bag and positioned out of direct sunlight at a constant 70°F (21°C) for up to two months, or slightly longer, for roots to establish.

The plastic bag may then be removed and the plant carefully weaned and grown on.

Seeds of citrus may also be germinated at a similar temperature when sown in a shallow pot or pan of seed and cutting compost. Germination may take just over a month, after which the clear plastic or glass cover may be removed and the seedlings carefully grown on. They should then be gently pricked out and potted up in 3½in (9cm) pots of potting compost.

CLERODENDRUM THOMSONIAE

Clerodendrum can be slightly difficult to grow even as a houseplant and is, therefore, somewhat more demanding in its needs when propagated.

From late spring to early summer cuttings measuring 4–6in (10–15cm) should be taken using a pair of secateurs or pruning shears. Each cutting should then be dipped into a hormone rooting powder and then inserted in a 3½in (9cm) pot of seed and cutting compost. Each cutting should then be covered with a clear plastic bag to conserve water and reduce transpiration and kept at a constant 70–72°F (21–22°C) for up to two months in reasonable light, but well away from direct sunlight.

Ideally, the cuttings would root better in a heated propagation unit, but if you are lucky and rooting is successful, the cutting will show signs of new growth. At this stage the plastic bag may be removed and the plant carefully weaned and grown on, feeding as necessary.

Once the plant has become more established with a good root system and framework of foliage, it can then be potted up into a 5in (13cm) pot of potting compost.

C

CLIVIA MINIATA

*C*livia can sometimes be rather difficult if only because it may result in a rather awkward process, requiring the removal of offsets that tend to be produced by the mother plant among a mass of strap-like leaves, bulbs and roots.

After the plant has finished flowering in late summer, remove the plant, or rather collection of plants, to gain greater access to the offsets.

By a process of gently teasing apart and cutting, remove any offsets that are large enough to pot up separately. These should consist of several leaves, at least three or four, measuring up to 10in (25cm). It is important during the separation process that a clean cut is made between the offset and the mother plant.

The offset should then be potted up in a 4¼–5in (11–13cm) pot using a peat-based potting compost, keeping the plant at a temperature of about 65–68°F (18–20°C) and maintaining a relatively dry regime in the compost. Only water sufficiently to keep the compost from drying right out. This will help to promote more rapid root establishment during the critical early stages.

Once sufficiently well rooted, the plant may then be grown on as normal.

CODIAEUM VARIEGATUM PICTUM

*T*he croton or codiaeum is a plant that requires a high level of care during propagation. Commercially grown crotons are propagated in heated propagation beds with a soil temperature of between 70–75°F (21–24°C).

From late spring and through the summer, the plant may be propagated from tip cuttings measuring 4–6in (10–15cm). More often than not the croton is grown as a single-stemmed plant and it will be necessary to wait until the plant is mature enough to produce side-shoots which are suitable for propagation.

Tip cuttings taken from side-shoots should be dipped into hormone rooting powder and inserted in a 3½–4¼in (9–11cm) pot of potting compost. This 'direct sticking' method means that, once the plant has been rooted, it can be grown on without having to have its new roots disturbed during the potting process.

Cover the cutting with a clear plastic bag and keep it at a temperature of 75°F (24°C) in a well-lit position, but out of direct sunlight.

After a period of up to two months, during which time the compost should be kept moist, the roots should be sufficiently well developed to allow the bag to be removed and the plant weaned and grown on.

Remove 4–6in (10–15cm) tip cutting.

Remove lower leaf or leaves.

Dip in hormone rooting powder and insert in 3½–4¼in (9–11cm) pot.

Cover with clear plastic bag.

C

COLEUS BLUMEI

*T*he coleus or flame nettle must really be one of the easiest and most rewarding plants to root, due to the ease of the propagation process. It may either be rooted by the direct sticking method or may be started off in water.

For the direct sticking method, simply gently pinch off tip cuttings measuring 2–3in (5–7.5cm) from mid-summer through to late autumn, taking care not to crush or bruise the delicate fleshy stem of the cutting.

Hormone rooting powder may be used to dip the cutting in, but it really is not necessary. The cutting should then be dibbled into a 3½in (9cm) pot of potting compost and kept at a temperature of 65–68°F (18–20°C) in a well-lit position, taking care not to allow the compost to dry out.

Rooting should take place within ten to fourteen days after which the plant may be grown on.

The cutting may also be started off in a clear container holding water in which the base of the cutting is placed. Keep the cutting at a similar temperature and environment out of direct sunlight: roots will quickly develop. When the roots are 2in (5cm) long, gently pot up the plant in a 3½in (9cm) pot of peat-based potting compost, taking care not to break off the relatively brittle roots. The plant may then be grown on as normal.

C

COLUMNEA BANKSII

Columnea may be propagated almost at any time from mid-spring to late summer.

As the plant naturally produces long trailing stems that occasionally need a trim to keep in check, it is worth taking advantage of this to generate cutting material for propagation.

Using a sharp knife, or a pair of secateurs or pruning shears, trim as required and select healthy tip cuttings measuring 3–4in (7.5–10cm). If necessary, pull off any lower leaves that may not be required and dip the cutting into a hormone rooting powder before direct sticking three cuttings to a 3½in (9cm) pot, or five cuttings to a 4¼in (11cm) pot, filled with a peat-based seed and cutting compost.

Keeping the compost hardly moist, the cuttings should root without needing to be covered at a temperature of 68°F (20°C), but if the atmosphere is dry it may be worth covering the cuttings with a clear plastic bag. After a month to six weeks of being kept warm and out of direct sunlight, the cuttings should have rooted sufficiently to allow the cover, if used, to be dispensed with and to be grown on accordingly.

As the cuttings start to grow it is important to start feeding as soon as possible after rooting to help build up a healthy, well-formed plant before winter conditions put the plant under stress.

C

CORDYLINE TERMINALIS

*T*he propagation of *Cordyline terminalis* may appear to be somewhat drastic as it usually involves the 'beheading' of the plant before further plants can be propagated.

Obviously this is most unwise to carry out until the plant begins to look rather elongated and possibly straggly. When this is the case cut off the top of the plant with a pair of secateurs or pruning shears to produce a 4–6in (10–15cm) shoot.

This should then be dipped into hormone rooting powder and inserted in a 3½in (9cm) pot of seed and cutting compost which should be adequately wetted, but not over-watered. Cover the cutting with a clear plastic bag and maintain a temperature of about 70°F (21°C), keeping the cutting in a moderately lit position.

At the same time as taking off the top shoot, sections of stem below the cut may be cut off into pieces measuring 2–3in (5–7.5cm) using the same technique, and taking care to ensure that each piece of stem has a bud on it.

After several weeks when rooting has taken place, remove the rooted cuttings from the cover and pot them up singly in a 4¼–5in (11–13cm) pot of peat-based potting compost.

Remove 4–6in (10–15cm) shoot.

Dip base of shoot in hormone rooting powder and insert in 3½in (9cm) pot of seed and cutting compost.

CROSSANDRA INFUNDIBULIFORMIS

Crossandra is propagated from mid-spring to early summer from tip cuttings removed with a sharp knife, or a pair of secateurs or pruning shears.

Tip cuttings measuring between 2–3in (5–7.5cm) should be selected to ensure that they are not too soft and lush. If possibly they should be beginning to form semi-hardened stem tissue. The cuttings should then be dipped into hormone rooting powder and inserted one per 2½in (6cm) pot filled with seed and cutting compost. Alternatively, up to five may be inserted in a 5½in (14cm) half-pot or pan.

Cuttings should then be covered with a clear plastic bag, and maintained at a temperature of 70–72°F (21–22°C) in a reasonably well-lit position out of direct sunlight, for a period of up to two months or as soon as rooting has taken place. The plastic cover may then be removed and the cuttings grown on a little more to harden off the plants before potting up.

When a reasonable root system has developed, in three to four months, moisten the compost in the pot or pan and gently remove the cutting, taking care not to damage the root system. Pot each rooted cutting individually in a 3½in (9cm) pot of potting compost.

CRYPTANTHUS

*T*he cryptanthus is one of the most extraordinary plants to propagate, ideally suited to the enthusiast who does not like to use a knife or other cutting tool.

In order to obtain propagation material all you virtually have to do is occasionally tap or shake a mature plant to loosen an offset. Offsets easily break off mature plants, whether from the base or from the top growth.

As rooting takes a very long time it is better to try to propagate in mid- to late spring to give the offset the summer months in which to root.

Simply lightly press the offset into a 2½–3½in (6–9cm) pot of seed and cutting compost, enclosing the offset in a clear plastic bag. Keep the offset at a temperature of 68–70°F (20–21°C) in a moderately lit position for three to four months. During this time it is imperative not to keep checking to see if rooting has started, as the disturbance will check the rooting of the plant.

Once rooted, feed the developing plant with a dilute solution of a liquid fertilizer, but do not pot on until the root system is more established, in around six months, because cryptanthus tends to produce a slow-growing, relatively weak root system that can be easily damaged.

CYCLAMEN PERSICUM

*A*lthough painstaking in terms of the effort and time required, a successfully propagated cyclamen in the home is well worth the trouble.

Seed may be sown either in late summer to flower in the late autumn and Christmas period in the following year or at any time from late summer through until spring to flower up to approximately 15 months later. Sow the seed in shallow pans or trays, using a seed and cutting compost and lightly covering the seed. Germinate at a constant 65–68°F (18–20°C), keeping the seed in the dark.

Check regularly for germination, which may take up to several weeks and normally appears rather patchily. As soon as the seedlings are seen to develop place the pan or tray in a well-lit position and grow on until large enough to handle. Maintain a temperature of 55–60°F (13–15°C) with a free-moving supply of air. Prick out the individual seedlings when large enough into 3½–4¼in (9–11cm) pots of peat-based potting compost and continue to grow on at 55–60°F (13–15°C). Avoid draughts, but ensure a good exchange of air to prevent a stuffy dank atmosphere which the cyclamen hates.

C

CYPERUS ALTERNIFOLIUS 'GRACILIS'

Cyperus is most easily propagated by division from mid-spring to early summer, although the ease with which this can be achieved may depend to some extent upon one's strength!

As the plant is normally kept growing by standing in water the compost should be moist: if it is not moist enough, water the plant well before removing it from its pot.

With a sharp knife, cut carefully through the mass of roots to separate clumps of at least four to five stems. To avoid root damage, try to separate the pieces by hand.

Once this has been achieved, simply pot up the clumps into a suitable size of pot such as 3½–4¼in (9–11cm), using a peat-based potting compost and taking care to water the plants well.

Whereas the technique of splitting up the clump may be applied to all cyperus it is possible to propagate *Cyperus alternifolius* 'Gracilis' by another unusual method as well. Flower heads may be used as propagation material by placing the flower head, with bracts cut back by one-third to one-half with a pair of scissors, and a section of stem attached measuring approximately 2in (5cm), in water or moist seed and cutting compost.

Once rooted, the plant may be potted up in a 3½in (9cm) pot of potting compost. During the process try to maintain a temperature of 68–72°F (20–22°C) and make sure that the plant is positioned in good light, but out of direct sunlight.

D

DIEFFENBACHIA AMOENA

Although a number of plants are poisonous it is worth taking particular care when handling the dieffenbachia. Before starting to propagate the plant, try to wear gloves and avoid all contact with the sap due to its poisonous and violently irritating effect. Remember also to wash your hands and exposed skin, and to clean tools after the procedure.

For the best results propagate dieffenbachia from mid-spring to early summer.

Tip cuttings of 4–5in (10–12.5cm) should be cut with a sharp knife and prepared by removing any lower leaves that would be buried in the compost. The cutting should then be dipped into a hormone rooting powder and inserted in a 3½–4¼in (9–11cm) pot of a peat-based seed and cutting compost.

The cutting should be covered with a clear plastic bag and kept out of direct sunlight at a temperature of 72–75°F (22–24°C) until rooted. This can take up to two months. Remove the bag from time to time to trim off any decaying leaves to avoid the spread of a fungal rot.

Once rooted, remove the bag and commence feeding before potting on when large enough into a 5in (13cm) pot of a peat-based potting compost.

Large overgrown dieffenbachias with long bare stems may also offer propagation material in the form of the stem. This may be cut into sections measuring about 3in (7.5cm) which are gently pressed into the surface of a peat-based seed and cutting compost and cared for in a fashion similar to the tip cuttings technique. Stems will normally produce one plant, but if you are lucky and two are generated, take care to divide the stem carefully and pot up each plant separately.

D

Stem Cutting

Cut stem carefully with sharp knife.

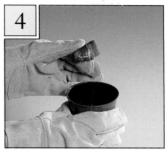

Dust lightly with hormone rooting powder.

Ensure cut is made cleanly.

Press gently onto compost surface.

Cut stem into 3in (7.5cm) pieces.

Ensure stem is not buried and cover with plastic bag.

Tip Cutting

Remove 4–5in (10–12.5cm) tip cutting.

Dip in hormone rooting powder, insert in 3½–4¼in (9–11cm) pot and cover with clear plastic bag.

D

DIONAEA MUSCIPULA

The diminutive Venus fly trap is not an easy plant to cultivate even when mature, and as such it can often be rather difficult to propagate. However, success achieved with this fascinating plant will be most rewarding.

With great care it is possible to separate the root gently from late spring to early summer. Ensure that the compost is moist and pot the root pieces in a 3½in (9cm) pot in a specialized mixture of sphagnum moss peat, sphagnum moss and, if possible, leaf-mould. Maintain a temperature of around 65–68°F (18–20°C) in moderate light. Covering the plant with a clear plastic bag or a glass bell jar may help it to propagate and develop more readily.

Alternatively, Venus fly trap may also be raised from seed sown in a similar material mixed in equal parts with sharp sand. The seed should be lightly covered, kept evenly moist and maintained at a temperature of about 70°F (21°C) until germination has taken place. Covering the seed tray or pan with a piece of clear plastic or glass will help to encourage germination.

When large enough to handle, prick out the seedlings and pot up singly, using the potting formulation, in 2½–3½in (6–9cm) pots.

DIPLADENIA SANDERI

As soon as dipladenia produces fresh new growth in the spring it is time to consider propagating it.

Tip cuttings measuring up to 3in (7.5cm) should be removed with a sharp knife and dipped into hormone rooting powder before being inserted in a 3½in (9cm) pot of seed and cutting compost.

Dipladenias are quite demanding of a high temperature to encourage rooting and you will need to maintain a temperature of up to 80°F (27°C) for successful rooting to occur. Covering the cutting with a clear plastic bag will help to conserve water in the leaf tissue.

Once rooted, the plastic bag may be removed, but continue to keep the plant in a moderately lit position.

If you wish to promote growth after rooting, the plant may be fed with a dilute liquid fertilizer. Eventually pot it up when large enough into a 4¼–5in (11–13cm) pot of a peat-based potting compost.

D

Cut stem with secateurs.

Cut stem into 2–3in (5–7.5cm) pieces.

Take care to keep stem right way up, dip into hormone rooting powder and insert in 3½in (9cm) pot. Cover with clear plastic bag.

DRACAENA MARGINATA

*D*racaena will grow to produce large, often multi-stemmed, plants that may need to be pruned to keep in check, an ideal time to consider propagation.

Dracaena may be propagated by tip or stem cuttings. Shoots produced from the base of the plant may also be used. Tip cuttings and shoots produced at the base of the plant should be removed with a sharp knife and trimmed to 4–6in (10–15cm).

Stem cuttings, consisting of the bare stem, should be cut with a pair of secateurs or pruning shears into 2–3in (5–7.5cm) pieces, taking care to ensure that each piece has a dormant shoot-bud. It is also important to ensure that the pieces of stem are kept the right way round; it can be very embarrassing to pot them upside down!

Dip each cutting into hormone rooting powder, stripping off any unwanted leaves and dibble each one into 3½in (9cm) pots of seed and cutting compost. Enclose the cuttings in a clear plastic bag at a temperature of 75°F (24°C) out of direct light. The compost should be kept barely moist.

After a period of up to two months rooting should have taken place. The bag should be removed as soon as the cuttings show signs of growth and start developing a reasonable root system.

The cuttings are then ready to be grown on and fed with a liquid fertilizer as required to help form a reasonable plant.

For the best results from propagating the plant it is worth avoiding the height of summer and to aim for propagating in mid- to late spring or late summer to early autumn.

Although quite different in form, dracaenas such as *D. sanderiana*, *D. fragrans* and *D. deremensis* may all be propagated similarly.

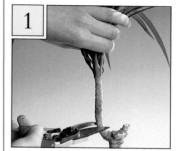

Remove 4–6in (10–15cm) tip cutting.

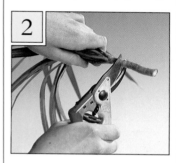

Dip into hormone rooting powder.

Insert in 3½in (9cm) pot, gently firm and cover with clear plastic bag.

E

ECHEVERIA SETOSA	*EPIPHYLLUM × ACKERMANNII*

The succulent plant echeveria is relatively easy to propagate by various techniques. The most popular is carefully to break or cut off a rosette or offset and simply insert it into a 2½in (6cm) pot of cacti and succulent compost, removing any lower leaves that are surplus and that may get in the way or rot.

The compost should be kept barely moist and at a temperature of around 68°F (20°C) for a period of up to a month, during which time the plant should start to root.

Alternatively, leaves that are almost mature but not too old, may be carefully removed by simply gently tugging sideways. Take care to select leaves that will not spoil the shape or appearance of the mother plant.

Dip the base of the leaf into hormone rooting powder and dibble into a half-pot or pan filled with cacti and succulent compost. Leave sufficient space between the leaf pads to enable them to be gently removed once rooted.

As with propagating from offsets, keep the leaf cuttings at 68°F (20°C) in reasonable, but not direct, light. Carry out the process in mid-spring to early summer for best results. Once rooted, which may take several weeks, gently prick out the leaf pads and pot them up in cacti and succulent compost in 2½in (6cm) pots.

The magnificent orchid cactus is probably best propagated from cuttings or side-shoots removed in mid-spring to early summer.

Cuttings or side-shoots should be carefully removed to avoid damage to the mother plant. Use a sharp knife to separate the offspring from the parent at the union between the main plant and the side-shoot.

The ideal size for cuttings is 4–6in (10–15cm) and these should be left for a day or so out of the light to allow the wound to start to form a callus.

The cutting should then be dipped into hormone rooting powder and inserted in a 3½–4¼in (9–11cm) pot of cacti and succulent compost. Maintain a temperature of 65–68°F (18–20°C) in moderate light, keeping the compost barely moist. Rooting should take place within a month, after which the plant may be grown on.

The orchid cactus may also be propagated from seed sown at 75–80°F (24–27°C) in a seed and cutting compost, pricking out the seedlings when large enough to handle to pot on. However, to obtain 'true' varieties cuttings should only be taken, for seed tends to produce a range of all of the varieties that make up the choice hybrids, some of which may not be worth growing in the home.

E

EPIPREMNUM AUREUS

Probably more commonly known under its former name of scindapsus, the epipremnum or Devil's ivy may be propagated quite easily in mid- to late spring even into early summer.

Tip cuttings measuring 3–4in (7.5–10cm) should be dipped into hormone rooting powder, taking care to remove the lower leaf after cleanly removing the cutting with a sharp knife. Scindapsus or epipremnum leaves are particularly susceptible to rotting and should be kept well clear of the compost.

Cuttings may be inserted singly into 2½in (6cm) pots of seed and cutting compost, and then potted up three to a 5in (13cm) pot of potting compost, removing any surplus compost from the cuttings to accommodate them. Altern-atively, three or four cuttings may be inserted in a 5in (13cm) pot of seed and cutting compost, and rooted and grown on, taking care to supplement nutrient requirements by feeding at an earlier stage than would be the case with the previous technique.

Either way, cover up the pot and cuttings with a clear plastic bag and keep in a well-lit position out of direct sunlight at a temperature of 70–75°F (21–24°C) for up to two months, after which the bag may be removed and the cuttings grown on.

It is also worth trying to root the cuttings by placing them in water, potting them up when the roots are about 2in (5cm) long. Take great care not to damage the roots because they can be very brittle.

E

EPISCIA DIANTHIFLORA

*T*he episcia is a plant that, under the right conditions of cultivation, constantly appears to regenerate new growth and is therefore reasonably easy to propagate.

During mid-spring to early summer, when the plant is more likely to tolerate disturbance, it may be propagated by division of the roots.

Although the technique may well be carried out without removing the plant from its pot, you may find it easier to achieve if you do remove it rather than struggling and risking damage to the cutting and the plant.

Moisten the compost and remove the plant from its pot and, taking a sharp knife, cut off a cluster of leaves together with the stolon (swollen root) to which it is attached, as well as whatever roots may be carefully removed.

Pot up the pieces either singly in 2½–3½in (6–9cm) pots of potting compost or three to five in a 5in (13cm) pot growing on at a temperature of 70–72°F (21–22°C) in reasonable light out of direct sunlight. Be sure to keep the compost moderately moist in the early stages of propagation, increasing the frequency of watering as and when appropriate.

E

Remove 3in (7.5cm) tip cuttings.

2

Dip in hormone rooting powder and insert in 5½in (14cm) half-pot.

EUONYMUS JAPONICUS 'ALBOMARGINATUS'

Tip cuttings of euonymus measuring up to 3in (7.5cm) may be propagated from mid-spring to early summer, using a sharp knife or pair of scissors to remove them cleanly.

The base of the stem should be dipped into hormone rooting powder and dibbled into a 5½in (14cm) half-pot filled with seed and cutting compost and covered with a clear plastic bag. The compost should be just moist and not too wet, or rotting will occur.

Maintain a temperature up to 70°F (21°C) for up to two months in reasonable light before removing the bag and growing on the plants a little more to produce a more developed root system. The rooted cuttings may then be carefully lifted and potted up singly in 3½in (9cm) pots of potting compost.

With variegated forms of this plant it is important to keep the stock true to form by not propagating any shoots that are reverting, thereby losing the colour and variegation. Even when plants are mature, it is important that reverting shoots should be trimmed off and disposed of as soon as they appear.

Insert two canes, one on either side of pot.

Cover with clear plastic bag.

EUPHORBIA MILLII SPLENDENS

The crown of thorns may be propagated from tip cuttings taken from mid-spring to early summer. However, the rate of success is usually rather small, with a high failure rate, so do not be too disappointed if at first you don't succeed.

Using a sharp knife or secateurs, taking care not to get pricked by the sharp spines or to get any of the poisonous milky sap on exposed skin, remove tip cuttings measuring 3–4in (7.5–10cm), and set to one side for a day or so to start to form a callus. Dip the cutting in hormone rooting powder and insert one per pot in a 2½in (6cm) pot of cacti and succulent compost, taking care to keep the compost barely moist. If excessive leakage of the white milky sap occurs, it may be stemmed by dipping the base into powdered charcoal or water.

Keep the cuttings in a well-lit position out of direct sunlight at around 70°F (21°C) for up to two months to allow rooting to take place. Cuttings that are not going to take will quickly dehydrate, wither and rot and should be removed. Once rooted, the cuttings should be grown on and potted up when growth becomes more vigorous, using a 3½in (9cm) pot of cacti and succulent compost.

E

EUPHORBIA PULCHERRIMA

The poinsettia may be propagated from mid-spring to early summer, to still allow time for the plant to grow sufficiently well to produce the characteristic red, pink or cream bracts.

Once the plant starts to produce new shoots these may be removed with a sharp knife as tip cuttings when approximately 3in (7.5cm) long.

Dip the cuttings into a hormone rooting powder and insert one per 2½in (6cm) pot of seed and cutting compost.

When grown commercially, water loss by transpiration of plants is reduced by misting regularly. This may be done in the home provided that you do not forget to do so, and that the mist is fine and is not allowed to saturate the compost. Alternatively, cuttings may be rooted under a clear plastic bag.

The cuttings should be kept in a well-lit position out of direct sunlight at a temperature of 70–72°F (21–22°C). Poinsettia cuttings will produce quite a pronounced callus within about two weeks and should be reasonably rooted within a month or so. Once the root system is well established, pot the rooted cutting up into a 3½, 4¼ or 5½in (9, 11 or 14cm) pot using a peat-based potting compost.

E

EXACUM AFFINE

*T*he compact-growing exacum may be propagated by seed sown in late winter to mid spring to produce plants that will flower in the same year in early to mid-autumn. Alternatively, seed sown in early autumn will flower in the following year in mid to late spring.

Sow the seed thinly in either a seed tray or 5½in (14cm) half-pot of seed and cutting compost at a temperature of around 70°F (21°C).

Once the seed has germinated and the seedlings are large enough to handle, moisten the compost and prick them out into 3½in (9cm) pots of a peat-based potting compost and grow on.

Take particular care not to over-water exacum, especially during the stage when the seedlings first develop as they can easily damp-off and be lost. Even after potting on try to take care with the watering, particularly in the early days while the seedlings become established.

FATSHEDERA LIZEI

*W*hile *Fatshedera lizei* may be rooted in a seed and cutting compost and potted on as required, it may be worth considering direct sticking to save time and hasten establishment and development.

From mid-spring to early summer take 3–4in (7.5–10cm) tip cuttings, as the plant starts to develop new growth, using a sharp knife or pair of scissors.

After having removed any surplus lower leaves, dip the cutting into hormone rooting powder and insert one per pot in a 3½in (9cm) pot. Alternatively put three per pot in a 4¼–5in (11–13cm) pot filled with a peat-based potting compost.

Cover the cutting with a clear plastic bag and to reduce water loss keep it in moderate light at a temperature of around 65–68°F (18–20°C).

Rooting should take place within a few weeks, provided the compost is not kept too moist; otherwise, the cutting will rot off. After rooting, remove the plastic bag and grow the plant on, taking care to allow the compost almost to dry out in between waterings as this will help to stimulate the development of the root system.

Remove 3–4in (7.5–10cm) tip cutting.

Dip in hormone rooting powder and insert in 3½in (9cm) pot.

Place clear plastic bag over cane supports.

Secure bag with elastic band.

Remove 3–4in (7.5–10cm) tip cutting.

FICUS BENJAMINA

*T*he weeping fig may be propagated from mid-spring to early summer, but you may need some patience in enticing it to root.

Tip cuttings measuring 3–4in (7.5–10cm) should be removed with a pair of secateurs or pruning shears and dipped into hormone rooting powder. As they are slow to root and easily put off, they should be inserted one per pot in a 2½in (6cm) pot of seed and cutting compost with a lower nutrient status than a standard potting compost which could inhibit rooting.

Covering the cuttings with a clear plastic bag may be useful, but is not essential provided the atmosphere is not too dry. The cuttings should be kept at a minimum of 70°F (21°C) and up to 75°F (24°C) for rooting to take place. This may take several weeks. Sudden leaf drop is a sure sign that something has gone wrong and that the propagation is failing.

However, if successful, the cutting should then be allowed to grow on and develop a healthy root system before being potted up into a 4¼–5in (11–13cm) pot of peat-based potting compost.

Dip in hormone rooting powder and insert in 2½in (6cm) pot of seed and cutting compost.

F

1

Remove 4–5in (10–12.5cm) tip or stem cutting.

2

Gently remove lower leaves from bottom 1–1½in (2.5–4cm) of stem.

FICUS PUMILA

*U*nlike many other varieties of ficus, the *Ficus pumila* or creeping fig is much easier to propagate, starting from mid-spring to early autumn, although cuttings taken earlier may propagate more readily.

Simply cut off tip or stem cuttings measuring about 4–5in (10–12.5cm) with a pair of scissors. The stems may be a little tough to cut with a knife without pulling up the roots if you are not careful.

Strip off sufficient lower leaves to allow 1–1½in (2.5–4cm) of stem to be inserted in the compost. Dip the lower stem into hormone rooting powder and insert five to seven cuttings in a 3½in (9cm) pot of peat-based seed and cutting compost, ensuring that the compost is reasonably moist. Cover the cuttings with a clear plastic bag and keep them at 65–68°F (18–20°C) in moderate light. Rooting will occur within a few weeks, with the appearance of new growth and even aerial roots signifying the event.

Remove the plastic bag and feed with liquid fertilizer until a well-formed plant is produced, after which it may be potted on into a 4¼in (11cm) pot or 5½in (14cm) half-pot filled with a peat-based potting compost.

3

Dip in hormone rooting powder.

4

Insert five to seven cuttings per 3½in (9cm) pot.

Tip Cutting

Remove 4–6in (10–15cm) tip cutting with at least three mature leaves.

$\mathcal{T}$he popular and easy-to-grow houseplant *Ficus robusta* requires a high rooting temperature to propagate successfully.

From mid-spring to mid-summer, cuttings consisting of a leaf and a piece of the main stem may be taken. This obviously means that the parent plant has to be pruned somewhat, a point worth considering before embarking upon the process.

Using a pair of secateurs or pruning shears, cut the stem into several pieces each with a leaf, leaving the stem approximately up to ½in (1cm) above the leaf and up to 2in (5cm) below it.

Wherever cut surfaces ooze the milky white latex, sprinkle powdered charcoal to help the sap congeal and wipe off any drops with a damp cloth before it becomes sticky and difficult to remove.

Taking each leaf and piece of stem, dip the stem into hormone rooting powder and insert it in a 2½in (6cm) pot of seed and cutting compost. Curl the leaf around a stick inserted vertically in the pot and secure it with a rubber band to support the cutting.

Dip into hormone rooting powder, having congealed oozing sap with powdered charcoal.

Insert tip cutting in 3½in (9cm) pot and cover with clear plastic bag.

Stem Cutting

Cut leaf with stem to allow about ½in (1cm) above leaf and 2in (5cm) below leaf.

Insert stem in 2½in (6cm) pot of seed and cutting compost.

Insert cane to provide support for leaf.

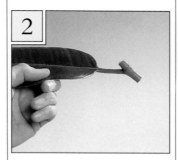

Dip base of stem in hormone rooting powder.

Gently firm cutting taking care not to bury leaf axil.

Place elastic band over slightly curled leaf to secure and cover with clear plastic bag.

Maintain a temperature of up to 80°F (27°C) in moderate light, using a clear plastic bag to cover the cutting as necessary to improve its humidity. The rooting process may take up to two months, After this time a new shoot will appear in the leaf axil. Following this the cutting may then be potted up in a 5in (13cm) pot of potting compost.

Alternatively, *Ficus robusta* may be air layered by selecting a length of shoot, ideally 6–10in (15–25cm), and cutting into the middle and then upwards for 2–3in (5–7.5cm).

The wound should then be eased open with moist sphagnum moss which should be inserted between the cut faces and packed around the cut area. Then wrap the shoot carefully and tightly, with clear plastic tied above and below the wound. After this the wrapped area should then be closely covered with kitchen foil to keep out the light.

After a period of about two months, the area should contain roots, provided that the moss has been kept moist. The shoot may then be cut off below the initial wound before being potted up in a 5in (13cm) pot of potting compost.

Air Layering

Select length of shoot 6–10in (15–25cm).

Carefully cut diagonally into stem.

Cut upwards in centre of stem for 2–3in (5–7.5cm).

Gently lever open wound taking care not to snap shoot off.

Insert match-stick at top of wound to hold open.

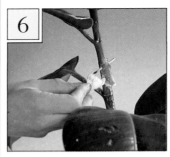

Dust wounded area with hormone rooting powder.

Gently place moist sphagnum moss between cut surfaces.

Remove match-stick and allow stem to flex back onto sphagnum moss.

Pack moist sphagnum moss around stem.

Gently compress sphagnum moss and wrap with clear plastic film.

Holding stem enclose sphagnum moss to form a "ball" around stem.

Secure plastic film with plastic covered tie at top and bottom.

Having applied ties to top and bottom check to ensure ties are secure, but not too tight.

Wrap aluminium foil around air layered area.

Form foil around area, gently crimping to secure as necessary.

Periodically check to ensure moss does not dry out, moistening as necessary by adding water through loosened top tie.

FITTONIA VERSCHAFFELTII

The snakeskin plant is a plant that is reasonably easy to propagate, but more difficult to cultivate than the smaller-leaved variety.

Cuttings may be propagated from mid-spring to early summer, removing cuttings measuring about 3–3½in (7.5–9cm) and consisting of at least two pairs of leaves. Use a sharp knife to produce a clean cut and avoid damage.

Dip the base of the stem of the cutting into hormone rooting powder and insert three cuttings in a 4¼–5½in (11–14cm) pot of peat-based potting compost.

Cover the cuttings with a clear plastic bag, allowing plenty of air space around the leaves to avoid them coming into contact with moisture on the plastic; otherwise, rotting will quickly occur.

Maintain a temperature of 68–70°F (20–21°C) in moderate light, keeping the compost just moist. Rooting should take place within a month or less, after which the plastic cover may be removed. Under better conditions of humidity it may be possible to root the cuttings without the need of a plastic cover, although unlike the mini snakeskin plant the larger leaves of this variety are more prone to dehydration.

F. VERSCHAFFELTII ARGYRONEURA 'NANA'

The diminutive mini fittonia or miniature snakeskin plant is much easier to propagate than the more brightly hued *Fittonia verschaffeltii*.

The low-growing trailing plant may be propagated from mid-spring to early autumn by carefully pinching or cutting off tip cuttings measuring about 3in (7.5cm). Each cutting should consist of at least three pairs of leaves if it is to take successfully.

Remove the lower pair of leaves and dip the base of the stem in hormone rooting powder before inserting five cuttings in a 3½in (9cm) pot of peat-based potting compost.

Cuttings may actually be rooted without having to be covered with a clear plastic bag, although this may help where problems of dehydration are encountered. Take care to ensure that the compost is not allowed to dry out, otherwise the cuttings will rapidly wither. Conversely, avoid over-watering, otherwise they are equally likely to succumb to rotting.

By maintaining them in a temperature of 65–68°F (18–20°C) in good light, but out of direct sunlight, rooting will take four to six weeks. After this the new plant may well be ready to take more tip cuttings from.

FUCHSIA SPECIES

*F*uchsia may be propagated with ease in mid- to late spring or early autumn from tip cuttings measuring 3–4in (7.5–10cm). Remove the cuttings with a sharp knife to avoid crushing the succulent fleshy stem, otherwise the cutting will quickly rot off.

Where possible, try to select tip cuttings that do not show signs of flowering. Remove flowers if necessary.

The cutting should then be dipped into hormone rooting powder and inserted one per pot in a 2½in (6cm) pot of seed and cutting compost. Although several cuttings may be inserted in larger pots, it may become more difficult to control any fungal rots that start to take hold.

A plastic cover placed over the cutting will promote more rapid rooting by reducing water loss from the thin leaves. This may be removed as soon as active growth starts. Once established, the cutting may then be potted up into a 4¼ or 5in (11 or 13cm) pot using a peat-based potting compost.

Alternatively, fuchsia may often be started in water, potting up the cutting when roots are about 2in (5cm) long. Maintain a temperature of 60–65°F (15–18°C) with good light conditions, but no direct sunlight during propagation.

GARDENIA JASMINOIDES

The gardenia is an acid-loving plant that hates lime and, as such, needs to be treated somewhat differently in terms of the type of compost used for propagation.

In mid- to late spring, remove 3–4in (7.5–10cm) tip cuttings with a pair of secateurs or pruning shears and dip the base of the stem in hormone rooting powder.

The cutting should then be dibbled into a 3½in (9cm) pot filled with a peat-based compost suitable for acid-loving, lime-hating plants. Enclose the cutting in a clear plastic bag and maintain it at a temperature of around 65–68°F (18–20°C) in a moderately lit position, taking care to ensure that the compost is kept reasonably moist but not over-wetted.

After a period of up to two months, rooting will occur and as soon as new growth is seen the plastic bag may be removed and the plant grown on.

During this critical period of development the plant may develop a condition known as chlorosis, which appears as yellow patches between green veins. This is normally due to a deficiency of iron which can be corrected by treating with sequestered iron.

When the plant has matured more it may be potted up into a 4¼–5in (11–13cm) pot filled with a peat-based compost suitable for plants that require a low pH. Where possible use a clay pot as this is more porous, allowing the compost to breathe.

G

GLORIOSA ROTHSCHILDIANA

The exotic *Gloriosa rothschildiana* grows to a rampant climbing lily which may be propagated very early in the year before the plant breaks into active and vigorous growth.

The lily-like plant may be propagated in very early spring. Start by gently removing the mother plant from the pot and then teasing apart the roots to expose the young tuberous growths. Take especial care not to damage the mother plant when disturbing the roots. It is best to remove the tubers with a sharp knife to ensure a clean separation.

Pot the tubers one per pot in a 4¼in (11cm) pot of a peat-based potting compost to grow on and develop at a temperature of between 65–68°F (18–20°C), feeding as the plant grows with a dilute liquid fertilizer.

As the plant grows it will also need to be potted up, probably into a 7in (18cm) pot. It will also require support for its long, relatively straggly stems.

Whenever possible, the plants should be raised in full light all of the time and they will tolerate periods of direct sunlight.

Gloriosa may also be germinated in mid-spring from seed sown at 65–68°F (18–20°C), and potted up accordingly as the seedlings develop.

GYMNOCALYCIUM MIHANOVICHII 'HIBOTAN'

This extraordinary cactus, which is produced as a novelty cactus with a bright chlorophyll (the green plant pigment) hue grafted onto another cactus rootstock, may be propagated with care by a keen enthusiast.

When the gymnocalycium at the top produces offsets large enough to remove (approximately 1in [2.5cm] in diameter), they may be removed carefully with a knife.

The offset should then be prepared by making a clean cut across the base. The size of the cut area should be reproduced on the 'stock' or the base plant which the 'scion' (top part) is to be grafted on to. Select a stock of *Hylocereus* spp. and cut across to ensure that the two cut surfaces of the stock and scion can be placed exactly together.

Upward cuts around the diameter of the stock may be made to reduce the diameter and to increase airflow.

The two plants may then be placed together and temporarily secured using toothpicks, rigid nylon bristles or cactus spines. The graft should then be covered with a clear plastic bag and kept at about 70°F (21°C) for up to two months.

Support materials may be carefully removed after about four to six weeks, but at all times great care must be taken not to disturb the union.

After about eight to ten weeks, the plastic bag may be removed and the plant grown on.

GYNURA SARMENTOSA

Gynura may be easily propagated in the home with very little special care. The plant may be propagated from early spring to late autumn, but usually greater success is experienced from mid-spring to early summer.

Remove tip cuttings measuring 3–4in (7.5–10cm) with a sharp knife and insert them directly in a 3½ or 4¼in (9 or 11cm) pot filled with a peat-based potting compost. Although there is no real need, hormone rooting powder may be used, but gynura normally roots readily without.

Dibble up to three cuttings into the pot and keep in a reasonably well-lit position out of direct sunlight at a temperature of around 65–68°F (18–20°C), keeping the compost reasonably moist, but not too wet.

Rooting will take place in about a month, after which the plant may be grown on, feeding as necessary.

Occasionally pinch out further tip shoots to keep the plant compact and to generate further propagation material.

HEDERA CANARIENSIS VARIEGATED

*T*he Canary Island ivy may be propagated from mid-spring to late summer, although plants propagated in the spring may establish themselves better.

When commercially grown, cuttings of the plant are taken from the long trailing stems and cut with sharp scissors to produce 4–5in (10–12.5cm) tip and stem cuttings. These are then direct stuck into 3½in (9cm) pots, three per pot, in potting compost and covered with clear plastic. Hormone rooting powder may be used, but is not essential. Keep the compost just moist, but not too wet or rotting will occur.

After about one month, the cuttings will have rooted. The plastic film may be removed and the cuttings grown on in good light (not direct sunlight) until more mature.

Alternatively, cuttings may be struck in water and allowed to develop roots measuring up to 2in (5cm) before being removed and gently potted up. In this instance, pot three per 3½in (9cm) pot, and five per 5in (13cm) pot.

Although ivies will happily grow in cool conditions, try to maintain a temperature of about 65–68°F (18–20°C) during propagation.

H

Remove 4in (10cm) tip or stem cuttings.

Insert five to seven cuttings per 3½in (9cm) pot and cover with a clear plastic bag.

HEDERA HELIX

The large and diverse range of *Hedera helix* or English ivy may be propagated quite similarly to *Hedera canariensis* variegated.

Tip or stem cuttings measuring about 4in (10cm) should be removed with a pair of scissors and direct stuck five to a 3½in (9cm) pot of potting compost. Keep the stem cuttings separate from the tip cuttings for greater uniformity. Cover the cuttings with clear plastic for up to a month to reduce water loss.

Again, hormone rooting powder may be used to dip the cuttings into before sticking, but this is not essential. Keep the compost barely moist for hedera can easily rot off if kept too wet at the root.

Alternatively, cuttings may again be struck first in water until 1½in (4cm) roots have developed before being potted up five to a 3½in (9cm) pot, or seven to nine in a 5in (13cm) pot.

One particular point to pay attention to is to ensure that the cutting is inserted in the compost the right way up. This might sound obvious, but it is very easy to insert the cuttings upside down. Leaves of hedera and also *Ficus pumila* tend to adjust themselves to the light whichever way the stem grows. To ease the problem, ensure that when the cuttings are taken, a longer stem is left below the lowest leaf and a shorter length of stem is left above the top leaf, as should be the case anyway for stem cuttings.

H

HEPTAPLEURUM ARBORICOLA

*T*he heptapleurum usually becomes rather lank and straggly in the home, an ideal time to consider propagation.

In mid- to late spring, prune back the plant as required with a pair of secateurs or pruning shears and cut into 7.5–10cm tip and stem cuttings.

Remove any surplus leaf and stalk that would otherwise be below soil level, then dip the base of the cutting into hormone rooting powder and insert it in a 3½in (9cm) pot of seed and cutting compost. Cover with a clear plastic bag and keep out of direct light at a temperature around 70°F (21°C) until new growth is evident, either at the top of the tip cutting or in the leaf axils of a stem cutting. The plastic bag may then be removed and the new plant grown on a little more, applying a liquid fertilizer to help the plant's development.

Once it is well formed, the plant may be gently removed from its pot and potted up in a 5in (13cm) pot of potting compost.

H

HIBISCUS ROSA-SINENSIS

*T*he hibiscus or rose of China may be propagated from mid-spring to late summer, as soon as the plant starts to produce new season's growth.

Try to select tip cuttings without signs of flowers and remove any with a sharp knife, or pair of secateurs or pruning shears. Alternatively, gently remove the cutting by pulling off a side-shoot complete with a heel, taking care not to tear off too much of the mother plant's bark.

Cuttings should measure about 3–4in (7.5–10cm) and should be dipped into hormone rooting powder before being inserted in a 2½–3in (6–7.5cm) pot filled with seed and cutting compost. They may then either be regularly misted or covered with a clear plastic bag and kept at around 70°F (21°C) in reasonable light out of direct sunlight.

As soon as the cuttings start to produce fresh growth, stop misting or remove the plastic bag and wean the plant, taking care to keep the compost just moist. Feed the plant with liquid fertilizer until it starts to form a good framework and then pot up in a 4¼–5in (11–13cm) pot containing a peat-based potting compost.

HIPPEASTRUM

*T*he amarylis can be propagated either from the tiny bulbs that are produced around the mother bulb or from seed. The latter method, of course, takes considerably longer to produce mature flowering bulbs.

After flowering and the die-back of leaves, the bulb may be carefully removed before being re-potted to start the new cycle of growth. Gently remove small bulbs that measure up to 1½in (4cm), using a sharp knife if necessary, to make a clean break which will avoid damaging the mother or offspring.

Pot up the new bulbs singly in 3½in (9cm) pots of a peat-based potting compost and grow on, potting up as required.

Seed may also be sown at about 70°F (21°C) in a 5½in (14cm) half pot of seed and cutting compost, pricking out and potting on singly as soon as large enough to handle.

It is important to remember that whereas young bulbs produced by the mother will come true to form, the seedlings will probably produce a myriad of colours typical of their mixed parentage.

HOWEA FORSTERIANA

Propagation of the howea, or what used to be called the Kentia palm, can provide the home enthusiast with a challenge.

As with the chamaedorea, a relatively high temperature is required, up to 80°F (27°C). Seed should be sown in mid- to late spring in trays or 5½in (14cm) half-pots or pans filled with seed and cutting compost, the compost just covering the seed.

The temperature should be maintained for many weeks as germination is very patchy and may take even up to two to three months or more. Keep the plant in light shade, with the compost just moist.

Germination is also poor and it is important to prick out seedlings as soon as they are large enough to handle.

Gently tease out the seedlings and pot up one seedling per 3½in (9cm) pot filled with a peat-based potting compost, growing on the new plant at a temperature of 68–70°F (20–21°C).

Grow the seedlings on in moderate shade. Keep the compost barely moist and take great care not to over-water.

H

HOYA BELLA

The *Hoya bella* or miniature wax plant is a superb trailing plant that can be propagated readily from mid-spring to late summer. As the plant is a succulent, it stores water in its tissue well, but still requires a relatively humid condition as it is an epiphytic (tree-living) plant originating from the rain forests.

Using a pair of sharp scissors, cut the trailing stems and make 3–4in (7.5–10cm) tip or stem cuttings, taking great care to keep the cuttings the right way round as it is easy to invert them and insert them upside down in the compost.

Having stripped off the lower leaves to expose about 1¼in (3cm) of stem, dip into hormone rooting powder and insert between five and seven in a 3½in (9cm) pot to form a well-shaped and 'full' plant. Pot tip cuttings and stem cuttings in separate pots to produce a uniform shape and use a peat-based seed and cutting compost to root and initially grow the plants in. Keep the compost barely moist.

Maintain a temperature of about 65–68°F (18–20°C) and enclose the cuttings in a plastic bag, venting occasionally to avoid excessive moisture build-up. Keep the cuttings in moderate light away from direct sunlight. Rooting is generally slow and takes up to two months, and even when the plant is mature the root system can be rather frail.

Once rooted, feed with a dilute liquid fertilizer, having removed and discarded the plastic bag. The plant will then grow to produce trailing growth, but do not consider re-potting for at least a year.

H

HOYA CARNOSA 'VARIEGATA'

*T*he variegated form of the wax plant, *Hoya carnosa* 'Variegata' is similar to propagate to the *Hoya carnosa* and *Hoya bella*, but due to its generally slower rate of growth and development warrants a little more care.

Having removed 4–5in (10–12.5cm) tip or stem cuttings with a pair of secateurs or pruning shears dip the base of the stem into hormone rooting powder. Insert three cuttings per 3½in (9cm) pot of peat-based seed and cutting compost, keeping the tip and stem cuttings separate for greater uniformity.

Cover with a clear plastic bag and maintain a steady 68°F (20°C) in moderate light, taking care not to over-moisten the compost, or premature death may result from rotting.

After about two months, roots should have developed sufficiently to enable new growth to start and for the plastic bag to be removed. Take particular care during the weaning process that the compost is not allowed to become too wet and is allowed almost to dry out in between waterings. Feed with a liquid fertilizer and grow on for at least a year before potting on into a peat-based compost.

H

HYPOESTES PHYLLOSTACHYA

Remove 3–4in (7.5–10cm) tip cutting.

Dip base of cutting into hormone rooting powder.

*T*he hypoestes (polka-dot plant) is a popular and common houseplant that can become rather straggly – a point in its favour as far as propagation is concerned.

From mid-spring to early autumn remove 3–4in (7.5–10cm) tip cuttings with a sharp knife or pair of scissors.

The cutting may either be dipped into hormone rooting powder and struck in a 2½–3in (6–8cm) pot filled with seed and cutting compost, or may be rooted in water. Either way remove any lower leaves that would be covered and root accordingly, keeping the cutting at 68–70°F (20–21°C) in reasonable light, but out of direct sunlight.

Cuttings rooted in compost will benefit from a plastic bag cover to reduce transpiration and encourage rooting, which should occur within two months. After rooting the bag may be removed and the cuttings weaned, and grown on, feeding with a liquid fertilizer until a reasonable plant is established. At this point pot up the cutting in a 4¼in (11cm) pot of a peat-based potting compost.

In the case of the cutting struck in water, pot up into a 3½in (9cm) pot when the roots are approximately 2in (5cm) long, taking care not to damage them during the potting process.

Hypoestes may also be propagated from seed sown in a seed tray, half-pot or pan filled with seed and cutting compost. Sow thinly in mid- to late spring, at 68–70°F (20–21°C), and prick out into 2½–3½in (6–9cm) pots of potting compost when large enough to handle.

Insert cutting in 2½–3in (6–8cm) pot of seed and cutting compost.

IMPATIENS PETERSIANA

The Impatiens, or Busy Lizzy, tends to become very untidy as it grows and, as with the hypoestes, it may well be worth producing new plants to replace older untidy ones.

Using a sharp knife to avoid damaging the succulent fleshy tissue, take tip cuttings measuring up to 3in (7.5cm) at any time from late spring to early autumn. Cuttings may be struck in water and then potted up into 3½in (9cm) pots of peat-based potting compost when the roots are about 1in (2.5cm) long, taking care not to damage them.

Alternatively, cuttings may be direct stuck into 3½in (9cm) pots in potting compost, having dipped the base of the stems in hormone rooting powder first.

Maintain a temperature of 65–68°F (18–20°C) and reasonable light, but not direct sunlight, in the early stages. Cuttings rooted in water first tend to root more readily with less losses than those struck in compost.

Impatiens may also be propagated from seed sown in mid-spring in half-pots, pans or seed trays at a temperature of 70°F (21°C). Seedlings should be pricked out with great care to avoid damage and potted up singly when large enough to handle, into 2½in (6cm) pots first, and then later into 3½ or 4¼in (9 or 11cm) pots in a peat-based potting compost.

JASMINUM POLYANTHUM

The indoor jasmine, or *Jasminum polyanthum,* really is a joy to propagate for the ease at which it can be done and the normally high strike rate. It also develops rapidly once rooting has established.

Although tip cuttings may be used, better results may probably be obtained using stem cuttings taken from late spring to early autumn consisting of a pair of leaves with at least 2in (5cm) of lower stem. The cutting should be removed with sharp scissors and 4in (10cm) tip cuttings and stem cuttings potted separately, with three to four cuttings inserted in a 4¼in (11cm) pot. The cuttings should be dipped into hormone rooting powder and struck in a peat-based potting compost, taking care to keep the compost moist, but not over-wetted.

Cover the cuttings with a clear plastic bag at a temperature of 65–68°F (18–20°C) until rooting occurs, when new growth suddenly starts to grow rapidly. Remove the plastic bag and grow on in a well-lit position, taking especial care not to allow the cuttings to dry out once the roots have established.

Feed with a liquid fertilizer and provide a framework support early on, before the plant becomes untidy and gets out of control. Pot up into a 5 or 7in (13 or 18cm) pot as necessary.

K

KALANCHOE BLOSSFELDIANA

*T*he popular flowering succulent *Kalanchoe blossfel-diana* is a relatively easy plant to propagate.

In mid- to late spring remove 3in (7.5cm) tip cuttings with a sharp knife. Then prepare them for propagation by leaving them for two or three days to start to form a callus, taking care to store them out of direct sunlight at a normal room temperature of 65–68°F (18–20°C).

The cuttings may then be gently inserted into 3½in (9cm) pots of cacti and succulent compost in reasonable light, but out of direct sunlight, at a temperature of 70–71°F (20–21°C). Take care not to allow the compost to become too wet, but keep it barely moist. As rooting occurs and the plant begins to grow, more water may be supplied, but still take care not to overdo it.

Take care, also, to ensure that any damaged or rotting tissue is removed as soon as possible before any disease spreads and affects other cuttings: something which can happen very quickly.

Remember towards the autumn that the plant must be exposed to short days and long nights; the short number of hours of daylight and long hours of darkness will encourage it to flower for the Christmas period.

KALANCHOE DAIGREMONTIANA

*I*f ever there was a plant that hardly needed any help with propagating itself, as well as having a tremendous capacity for reproduction, it has to be the *Kalanchoe daigremontiana* or Devil's backbone.

Although by no means a spectacular plant, this extraordinary novelty reproduces itself by producing tiny plantlets on the leaf edges with as many as 30 per leaf.

The plantlets grow and develop roots while still attached to the parent and, when large enough, approximately ¼in (½cm) across, they simply drop off. At this point help may be provided by gently potting the tiny plantlets either singly into 2½in (6cm) pots of cactus compost (which are actually too large!) or better still to pot a number of them into a 5½in (14cm) half-pot of cactus and succulent compost until about 1in (2.5cm). They may then be potted up singly in 3½in (9cm) pots of cacti and succulent compost, keeping them barely moist and almost drying out between waterings. Grow on at a temperature of 65–68°F (18–20°C) in a well-lit position.

Finally, beware of growing the plant too near other plants in your collection. Plantlets tend to fall off and grow almost anywhere with hardly any assistance at all!

LAURUS NOBILIS

*T*he bay tree is worth persevering to propagate, despite the plant's slow growth rate.

In mid- to late spring or late summer to early autumn, remove 4in (10cm) tip cuttings with a pair of secateurs, discarding any lower leaves to allow at least 1½–2in (4–5cm) of lower stem to be inserted in the compost.

Dip the base of the stem in hormone rooting powder and insert one cutting per pot in a 3½in (9cm) pot of seed and cutting compost. Keep the cutting in good light, but out of direct sunlight, at a temperature of around 65–68°F (18–20°C) until rooting has taken place, which may take from four to six weeks.

Once roots start to develop, commence liquid feeding. If the cutting was taken in spring consider repotting it in late summer into a 5in (13cm) pot of potting compost. However, if the cutting was taken in late summer to early autumn do not consider repotting until mid- to late spring in the following year.

Although cuttings prefer to be struck in compost that is relatively moist, do not keep the compost too wet. This is important as the plant develops as it may be over-watered, especially over the winter months.

Remove 4in (10cm) tip cutting.

Gently remove lower leaves to allow 1½–2in (4–5cm) of bare stem.

Dip base of stem in hormone rooting powder.

Insert tip cutting in 3½in (9cm) pot of seed and cutting compost.

LITHOPS

The extraordinary and diminutive lithops or living stones is a most unusual succulent. In appearance it closely resembles small pebbles scattered liberally in the pot of compost.

Although its rate of growth is quite slow, it can in time grow to almost fill the pot in which it is growing, resulting in all of the plants looking somewhat crowded.

In late spring or early summer the collection of plants should be gently removed from its pot and the tiny plants teased apart. Take particular care not to tear the roots or to bruise or crush the plants' fleshy tissue as you separate them.

Pot them either singly in a 2½in (6cm) pot, or in small numbers in a 3½in (9cm) pot of cacti and succulent compost with a small amount of shingle or gravel on top to improve the cosmetic appearance.

Take particular care with watering, and keep the compost barely moist, to allow the separated plants to develop new roots and become well established. Keep the plants at about 65–68°F (18–20°C) and grow them in a well-lit position with exposure to some hours of sunlight a day; otherwise, the tissue can become too soft and the plants can etiolate.

Lithops may also be propagated from seed sown in mid- to late spring at 68–70°F (20–21°C), pricking out seedlings when large enough to handle. A half-pot or pan is ideal for germinating the seed, using a cacti and succulent compost. However, it takes a number of years by this method to produce mature plants.

Moisten compost and gently remove plant from pot.

Gently separate plant into distinct clumps.

Tease apart clumps taking care not to damage roots by tearing.

Possibly better known as rabbits' tracks or prayer plant, the maranta is a plant that thrives in conditions of high humidity. This fact needs to be particularly borne in mind when propagating the plant.

Propagating may be carried out by either the division of a mature, well-formed plant that may be getting over-crowded, or by taking cuttings.

Propagation by division is probably the easiest technique, with the greater chance of success. In mid- to late spring ensure that the compost is moist, and remove the plant from its pot. Tease apart and cut with a sharp knife the roots of the plant, separating pieces complete with root that can be potted up on their own.

Pot up in a 3½–4¼in (9–11cm) pot of peat-based potting compost and cover with a clear plastic bag to improve humidity for the plant to accelerate successful establishment. Keep the plant at 70°F (21°C) out of sunlight in a moderately lit position in light shade.

Alternatively, take cuttings up to 4in (10cm) long and dip into hormone rooting powder, potting relatively shallowly in a 3½in (9cm) pot of peat-based seed and cutting compost. Treat in the same way as for plants that have been split up, removing the plastic bag after up to two months. Cuttings may be taken in early to mid-summer and, when rooted, should be fed with a liquid fertilizer until such time that the plant is mature enough to be potted up in a 4¼in (11cm) pot of peat-based potting compost.

Maranta leuconeura erythroneura is treated similarly, but tends to be more delicate and subject to a higher failure rate.

Carefully remove any dead or damaged roots and surplus compost.

Pot up plant in 3½–4¼in (9–11cm) pot.

Gently firm compost and cover plant with clear plastic bag.

MONSTERA DELICIOSA

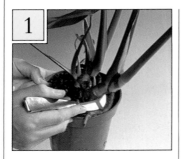

Place in 5in (13cm) pot and fill with peat-based seed and cutting compost taking care not to bury leaf axil.

Use cane to support, securing loosely with wire twist tie and cover with clear plastic bag.

Remove a growing point with at least two to three adult leaves.

Dip base of stem into hormone rooting powder.

The trouble with the monstera, commonly known as the Swiss cheese plant or Mexican breadfruit plant, is that in time it really can become a monster, and attempts to restrain it may finally result in the need to start off a new plant and discard the old.

Sever the growing point with two to three adult leaves, using a sharp knife, and pot it in a 5in (13cm) pot of seed and cutting compost. Use a cane and appropriate twist-tie or string to support the cutting, otherwise it will fall over. Pot just below the surface, ensuring that the growing point is fully exposed and not buried.

Maintain a temperature of 70°F (21°C) in moderate light, taking care to improve the humidity level by covering the plant with a clear plastic bag.

Mid-spring to early summer is probably the best time to carry out this process, enabling the cutting to establish during the late summer months. The plastic bag may be removed as soon as the plant starts to grow, at which time liquid feeding should be regularly carried out. Another method of propagation is layering, encouraging the plant to root its aerial roots into a new pot of compost and then severing the new part of the plant from the old.

The seed may also be propagated at 70–75°F (21–24°C), sown in a seed tray or pan filled with seed and cutting compost. Prick out the seedlings initially into 3½in (9cm) pots of potting compost and then grow on before potting up as required.

NEOREGELIA CAROLINAE 'TRICOLOR'

*T*he colourful neoregelia may be treated in a similar way to the aechmea.

Propagation is relatively straightforward, but requires great care to ensure that you do not damage and, therefore, possibly increase the chance of losing the offsets when they are produced.

Start work in mid- to late spring. Choose a plant with offsets measuring approximately 6–8in (15–20cm) having moistened the compost thoroughly first. Tease away some of the compost to expose the lower root of the offset and, using a sharp knife, make a clean cut close to the mother plant.

The offset may then be potted in a peat-based seed and cutting compost complete with as much as possible of its root system into a 3½–4¼in (9–11cm) pot. For the first month, or even up to two months, enclose the offset in a clear plastic bag and keep it at 70°F (21°C) in reasonable light, but out of direct sunlight.

Once the root system starts to develop, the plant may be removed from its cover and grown on, feeding with a reduced-strength liquid fertilizer both onto the compost and into the central vase, ensuring that water is also applied in the same way when the plant needs watering.

As the young plant develops, it may be potted up into a 5in (13cm) pot in late spring, probably the season after, in order to give it sufficient time to establish before the autumn and winter.

NEPHROLEPIS EXALTATA

The nephrolepis may be propagated by two techniques, the first being probably much more practical and effective than the latter.

As the plant produces runners complete with little plants which form at the end when the runner touches compost, this technique may be utilized to propagate new plants.

Active runners may be laid onto compost and young plants should form as the runner begins to root. When this occurs the runner may then be cut off and the young plant grown on.

This technique may be carried out whenever the plant is in active growth and particularly during the spring and summer. 3½in (9cm) pots filled with seed and cutting compost or potting compost are acceptable, taking care to ensure that the compost is kept reasonably moist.

Try to maintain a reasonable level of humidity and a temperature of around 65–68°F (18–20°C).

Alternatively, and more complicatedly, nephrolepis may also be propagated from spores produced on the undersides of the fronds. Collect the spores as they mature and are released on a white sheet of paper. Sow them very thinly onto the surface of seed and cutting compost lightly filled and even in a seed tray or half-pot or pan.

Cover with a sheet of clear plastic, glass or polythene and keep at 70°F (21°C) until germinated, which tends to be relatively poor, slow and patchy. When the young ferns are large enough to handle at ½–1in (1–2.5cm) prick them out and pot them up singly in 2½in (6cm) pots of potting compost and thereafter, when more developed, into 3½–4¼in (9–11cm) pots. Always keep out of direct light, and water from below by gentle and partial immersion.

P

PACHYSTACHYS LUTEA

*I*n mid- to late spring, when the pachystachys starts to produce new growth, the plant may be propagated from tip cuttings.

With a sharp pair of scissors, cut off side-shoots that measure up to 4in (10cm), having removed lower leaves to leave up to 2in (5cm) of bare stem at the base. Dip the cuttings into hormone rooting powder.

The cuttings may then be inserted one per pot in a 2½in (6cm) pot of seed and cutting compost, dibbling a hole in the moistened compost prior to inserting the cutting.

A clear plastic bag should then be placed over the cuttings and a temperature of 68–70°F (20–21°C) maintained. Rooting may take anything from a few weeks to up to two months to get established. Remove the plastic bag as soon as fresh growth starts to develop. Keep the cutting in a well-lit position, initially out of direct light until the plant is beginning to grow.

Having weaned the cutting and grown it on to a larger size, feeding as necessary with a liquid fertilizer, the young plant may then be potted up. Pot on into a 4¼–5in (11–13cm) pot of a peat-based potting compost, keeping the compost reasonably moist, but not too wet, and growing on in a well-lit situation.

P

PANDANUS VEITCHII

Surprisingly, the pandanus or screw pine is not as easy to propagate as one would imagine, though it repays careful attention. The plant's tough-looking leaves are, in fact, quite sensitive to a dry environment and during propagation, without effective care, they can turn brown at the tips and edges.

Carefully remove the offsets which appear as sucker-like shoots at the base of the plant; use a sharp knife to sever them cleanly from the parent. Do not remove growths that are too small as these may be more difficult to propagate. They should then be dipped in hormone rooting powder and inserted in a 3½in (9cm) pot filled with a seed and cutting compost.

Cover the young plant with a clear plastic bag and maintain a temperature of 68–70°F (20–21°C), exposing the plant to a reasonable level of light, but out of direct sunlight to prevent scorch.

Rooting may take up to two months, after which the bag may be removed. It is essential at this point to ensure that the atmosphere remains humid as the leaves of the pandanus may have become more susceptible to a dry environment; so be prepared to mist regularly or improve humidity in some other way.

The time of year is also important. As the propagation period is relatively lengthy it is worth starting in mid-spring to enable the plant to be propagated by early summer and possibly even potted into a 5in (13cm) pot, using a potting compost, by early autumn.

PASSIFLORA CAERULEA

The passion flower is a rapid-growing plant which produces long climbing stems capable of providing many cuttings per year.

In early to mid-summer stem cuttings may be taken using a sharp pair of scissors to remove them in 4in (10cm) pieces.

Discard any surplus lower leaf and dip the base of the stem into hormone rooting powder. The cutting may then be inserted in a 3½in (9cm) pot of seed and cutting compost and covered with a clear plastic bag. Maintain a temperature of 65–68°F (18–20°C) for up to a month, when rooting should have taken place.

The plant may be removed from the bag as soon as it starts to produce new growth, from which time it may then be regularly fed with a liquid fertilizer.

Continue to grow the new plant in a well-lit position until late autumn to early winter when watering should be drastically reduced to almost nothing. Just water enough to prevent dehydration.

In early spring the new plant may then be potted up into a 5in (13cm) pot of potting compost and grown on. Further repotting into a 7in (18cm) pot may be required later in the year in early to mid-summer although, where possible, it may be better to leave this until the following spring.

PELARGONIUM SPECIES

*T*he numerous pelargoniums may be propagated quite readily from early to late summer.

Tip cuttings measuring up to 4in (10cm) may be removed with a sharp knife dipped into hormone rooting powder. After having removed any lower leaves at the base of the stem, simply insert the cuttings in a 3½in (9cm) pot of seed and cutting compost.

There is no need to cover the cuttings, but take care to avoid dehydration by keeping them out of direct sunlight in a moderately lit position. The compost should not be wetted too much and should really be hardly moist, but obviously not dry.

The cuttings should start to root well within a month, but then need to be weaned to allow the young developing plants to be grown on eventually in full light, continuing to maintain a temperature of about 65°F (18°C).

As the plant starts to grow and on inspection the root–ball is found to be sufficiently well developed, the plant may be potted up into a 5in (13cm) pot, using a peat–based potting compost. Take equal care with the watering at this stage, being cautious not to over-water the plant; allow the compost to get on the dry side before rewatering.

PELLAEA ROTUNDIFOLIA

The diminutive and low-growing button fern is not a plant one would readily expect to propagate easily. However, it can be propagated either from spores or from the rhizome, a swollen stem-like growth that produces fronds and roots.

In mid- to late spring, when the plant starts to produce fresh growth, moisten the compost well and remove pieces of rhizome complete with fronds and roots. Use a sharp knife and take care to remove pieces of a manageable size as well as not to damage any part of the cutting. You may find it useful to remove the plant from its pot to gain greater access during this procedure.

The pieces of rhizome may then be lightly potted close to the surface of the compost and only just buried, using a peat-based potting compost, in a 3½in (9cm) pot. Keep the new plant at a temperature of around 68°F (20°C) and continue to maintain a high level of humidity, especially during the initial stages. A clear plastic bag may be used initially, but dispensed with after a couple of weeks or so.

Continue to grow the fern in moderate light away from direct exposure to the sun.

Alternatively the plant may also be grown from spores germinated in a similar fashion to the asplenium and nephrolepis, as described earlier.

P

PEPEROMIA CAPERATA

*A*lthough the *Peperomia caperata* may be propagated from tip cuttings in a similar way to several varieties of peperomia it is not really the best technique to use, especially with small plants. A far better technique is that of simply removing leaves complete with the leaf stem from mid-spring to mid-summer. Select fully formed leaves, not old ones, and cut cleanly with a very sharp knife. Trim the leaf stem to about 1–1¼in (2.5–3cm), again using a very sharp knife and taking great care not to crush the leaf stalk.

The leaf should then be dibbled into a seed and cutting compost in a tray or pan, using a small dibble or stick to allow its easy insertion into the compost. Do not compress the compost, but settle it with a light watering. The leaf should be just touching the compost and not buried.

Maintain a temperature of 68°F (20°C) in reasonable light, but not in direct sunlight, and take care to remove any leaves that start to rot before the infection spreads.

The cuttings will probably take up to two months to root. At the base of the leaf where it joins the leaf stalk, a new plant should form and when this is large enough to handle, at about 1¼–2in (3–5cm), it may be gently pricked out and potted up. Pot into a 3½in (9cm) pot using a peat-based potting compost, and grow on.

Select mature, but not old leaf and remove cleanly at base of leaf stem.

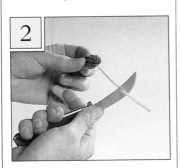

Trim leaf stem to about 1–1¼in (2.5–3cm).

Dip into hormone rooting powder and, gently holding by leaf, insert in 5½in (13cm) half-pot of seed and cutting compost.

P

1

Remove 3in (7.5cm) tip cuttings.

PEPEROMIA MAGNOLIAEFOLIA

*T*he variegated *Peperomia magnoliaefolia* or desert privet has thick glossy, fleshy leaves which help the plant to be propagated quite easily.

In mid-spring to early autumn the plant may be propagated from tip or leaf and stem cuttings.

Tip cuttings of 3in (7.5cm) may be taken with a sharp knife and directly stuck into a 3½in (9cm) pot of seed and cutting compost, having first been dipped into hormone rooting powder. The cutting should be kept at 65–68°F (18–20°C) in good light and initially out of direct sunlight. It is best to keep the compost just moist, and if anything on the dry side, in order to encourage rapid rooting.

Tip cuttings use rather a lot of plant material, whereas leaf and stem cuttings are a very effective way of increasing the stock of the plant. Sections of stem may be cut into pieces, each with a leaf attached.

Dip the piece of stem into hormone rooting powder and dibble into a 2½in (6cm) pot of seed and cutting compost. Keep the compost barely moist, if anything on the dry side, and maintain a temperature of around 68°F (20°C) in good light.

Within six to eight weeks rooting should take place and, in the case of the leaf and stem cutting after several more weeks, may be potted up in a 3½–4¼in (9–11cm) pot of peat-based potting compost.

2

Insert cutting in 3½in (9cm) pot of seed and cutting compost.

P

PERSEA AMERICANA

*B*etter known as the Avocado Pear, propagation of this plant is really a matter of curiosity.

Having removed the stone, clean it to ensure that no remnants of the fruit adhere which could rot. Once cleaned, the stone may be germinated on water or in compost.

To germinate on water, use a small jar or tumbler and position the avocado stone so that the rounded end is just in contact with the water. To achieve this you can either use matchsticks to wedge the stone, or simply use wire twist-tie to secure to the jar or tumbler, using a fairly heavy gauge of twist-tie. Take care to form the twist-tie into a loose collar near the base as a support; if fitted around the stone too tightly it could interfere with germination by constraining the shoots as the stone swells and splits.

Maintain a temperature of about 70°F (21°C) until germinated and then pot up into a 3½in (9cm) pot of seed and cutting compost, taking care not to damage the roots and ensuring that about one third of the stone is above the surface of the compost.

Alternatively, pot up a stone in a similar way using seed and cutting compost in a 3½in (9cm) pot and germinate at about 70°F (21°C) in reasonable light, once again ensuring that the top, more pointed end is uppermost, with about one third exposed above the compost.

When the plant has grown to about 8–10in (20–25cm) it may be potted up into a 7½in (18cm) pot.

1

Remove 4in (10cm) tip cuttings.

2

Dip base of stem into hormone rooting powder and insert in 5in (13cm) pot.

PHILODENDRON 'RED EMERALD'

Despite the size of the leaves of the *Philodendron* 'Red Emerald' it is possible to propagate them in the home.

However, due to the size of the plant it is best to use a larger-sized pot, obviously potting fewer cuttings per pot than one would with smaller-leaved philodendrons.

In late spring or early summer take tip cuttings measuring about 4in (10cm), using a sharp knife, and insert two, or possibly three if the leaves are not too large, in a 5in (13cm) pot of seed and cutting compost. Hormone rooting powder may be used to dip the lower part of the stem in before inserting the cutting. Enclose the cuttings in a clear plastic bag and maintain a temperature of about 68°F (20°C) in moderate light, keeping the compost moist.

After about one month rooting should have occurred, and new growth should appear. It is possible that during this period the aerial roots will start to grow quite actively.

The plastic cover may then be removed and the plant grown on, feeding as necessary with a liquid fertilizer to supplement the low nutrient status of the compost. Provide support as soon as required in the form of a moss pole or similar and pot up towards late summer into a 7in (18cm) pot using a peat-based potting compost if the plant is growing vigorously enough.

Philodendron 'Red Emerald' may also be propagated from stem cuttings, although the size of mature leaves may make this awkward.

3

Enclose with clear plastic bag.

PHILODENDRON SCANDENS

The popular climbing sweetheart plant, *Philodendron scandens* is one of the easier philodendrons to propagate successfully.

Once rooted, however, it is not very tolerant of disturbance, and it is therefore better to strike the cuttings in the pot in which they are to grow on in. Although the concentration of nutrients is lower in a seed and cutting compost, it is a more suitable medium to strike the cuttings in. Nutrients can always be supplemented after rooting with a liquid fertilizer.

Tip cuttings measuring 3–4in (7.5–10cm) may be removed with a sharp knife and inserted three to five to a 3½in (9cm) pot filled with seed and cutting compost. The base of the cuttings should first have been dipped in hormone rooting powder.

Keeping the compost reasonably moist, but not over-wetted, maintain a temperature of around 68°F (20°C) in moderate light, covering the cuttings with a clear plastic bag to improve humidity and reduce transpiration.

Within a month or so rooting should have taken place, and the plastic bag removed. Feed regularly with a liquid fertilizer and grow on, providing support as required.

Cuttings may be taken at any time from mid-spring through until early autumn, although plants produced earlier in the season will probably form more compact and better-shaped specimens.

Remove 3–4in (7.5–10cm) tip cuttings.

Dip base of stem into hormone rooting powder and insert three to five cuttings per 3½in (9cm) pot.

Insert two canes in pot for support.

Cover cuttings with clear plastic bag.

P

Remove 2½–3in (6–7.5cm) tip cuttings.

Gently remove lower leaf and dip into hormone rooting powder.

PILEA CADIERI

Pilea is very easy to propagate: within a few weeks it is possible to produce a plant of worthwhile proportions. Although feasible to propagate from late spring to the end of summer it is better to propagate in mid- to late spring to produce a reasonable plant in a shorter time.

Pilea has a relatively low nutrient requirement; so it is possible to direct stick cuttings into a pot filled with seed and cutting compost. Using a sharp knife or pair of scissors, remove 2½–3in (6–7.5cm) tip cuttings. Dip the bottom of the stem into hormone rooting powder and insert five to a 3½in (9cm) pot. Although it is not essential to cover the cuttings, this may be carried out to help improve their chances of taking if problems are encountered.

Maintain a temperature of 65–68°F (18–20°C) in a moderately lit position, keeping the compost hardly moist. Water when the compost begins to look dry, but do not allow it to dry right out or, conversely, to stay too wet.

Once rooting has started, within about a month, start to feed with dilute liquid plant food, increasing the rate to normal concentration after a further month or so.

To encourage the plant to become more compact and bushy the cuttings may be pinched back to help initiate the production of side-shoots.

Gently dip cuttings into pot filled with seed and cutting compost.

Insert five cuttings per 3½in (9cm) pot.

P

PLATYCERIUM BIFURCATUM

The platycerium or stagshorn fern is not one of the easiest plants to propagate, but successful results merit the care and expertise required. There are two ways to increase stock of the plant.

Mature platycerium sometimes produces a further plant that grows alongside the main plant. With great care the small plant may be very gently and expertly teased away from the mother plant, ensuring that the compost is moistened before starting the procedure. It is absolutely essential not to be too heavy-handed for fear of damaging the main plant and, if there is any belief that the mother plant could be damaged, it is better not to attempt the operation.

Once separated, carefully repot the mother plant and pot up the new plant in a peat-based seed and cutting compost. Covering the plant with a clear plastic bag for a few weeks may help it to establish faster, but this is not essential.

However, maintain a temperature of around 68°F (20°C) in reasonable but not direct light, at least for the first few weeks. Also try to keep the compost quite moist and do not allow it to dry out.

Platycerium may also be successfully propagated from spores collected from the underside of the fronds on pieces of plain paper.

These may be sown very thinly in a seed tray or pan filled with seed and cutting compost. Cover it with clear plastic, glass or polythene and keep it at 70°F (21°C) until the spores have germinated. When large enough to handle, prick them out and pot them up separately in 2½in (6cm) pots of seed and cutting compost.

When more mature, the plants may be attached to a piece of bark. Pack them with sphagnum moss and compost to produce a good base for the plant.

R

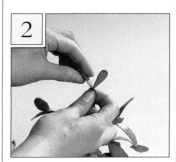

RHIPSALIDOPSIS ROSEA

*T*he rhipsalidopsis really needs little help in propagating itself and may be multiplied quite easily.

Although it may be propagated from mid-spring to early autumn, it is beneficial to propagate from mid-spring to early summer in order to give the new plant longer to become established before the winter.

Remove leaf pads from the mature plant by hand. Gently pull the pads off, taking care not to damage any tissue by any clumsy tearing action. Single or double pads may be removed as propagation material and these should be allowed to form a callus for a day or so out of direct light.

Having inserted the base of the leaf pad in hormone rooting powder dibble one to three pads in the centre of a 3½in (9cm) pot of peat-based seed and cutting compost or cacti and succulent compost. Maintain a temperature of 65–68°F (18–20°C) in moderate light initially until rooted, keeping the compost hardly moist.

Once rooted, move the plant to a position in a little more light, but out of direct sunlight, and water a little more frequently, taking care not to keep the compost too moist and to over-water.

If at any stage any of the leaf pads show signs of excessive dehydration by withering or any sign of rot, remove them and dispose of them before any disease organism can infect other plants.

Schlumbergera may also be propagated in the same way.

Gently remove leaf pads by holding between thumb and forefinger.

Carefully twist half a turn and gently pull off.

Dip base of pad into hormone rooting powder.

Ensure callus is coated with hormone rooting powder.

SAINTPAULIA IONANTHA

Although the African violet or saintpaulia may be propagated by division as well as from seed, the best method is to root leaves of the plant. It may be propagated by leaf cuttings throughout the year, but the most successful time is from mid-spring to early summer.

Select a well-formed, but not too young or, for that matter, too old leaf and remove it as close to the base of the rosette of leaves as possible. This may be done by gently holding the leaf stalk between the thumb and the first two fingers as close to the base as possible. Give the stem half a turn and a sharp tug and it should come away cleanly.

Taking a sharp knife, trim the leaf stem to 1–1½in (2.5–4cm) and thereafter hold the leaf by the leaf blade rather than the stalk. The leaf should be dipped into hormone rooting powder and inserted in a 2½in (6cm) pot of seed and cutting compost, dibbling a hole for the stem of the leaf first before insertion. Take care that the leaf blade does not touch the compost and leave an air space of about ¼in (1cm) left at the base of the leaf. Gently secure it by pushing compost around the stem. On no account firm it as bruising or crushing of the leaf stem will cause it to rot.

Leaves may also be propagated by inserting a number in a seed tray or up to four or five in a 5½in (14cm) half-pot.

Cover the leaf with a clear plastic bag and maintain a temperature of 70–75°F (21–24°C) in moderate light. Rooting may take up to six weeks, after which the cutting should be left for a further period of up to a further four to six weeks to encourage the cutting to produce plantlets. During this period keep the compost barely moist and do not over-water, otherwise rotting will quickly occur.

Carefully wean the plantlets by increasing the ventilation in the bag, and then gently tease the individual plantlets apart when they are about 2½in (5cm), taking care to handle them very gently.

Pot each plantlet singly into a 3½in (9cm) pot of peat-based potting compost and grow on. Do not pot more than one plantlet per pot or the plant will form a double or multi-crown which can look untidy in the initial stages.

1

Gently remove mature but not too old leaf.

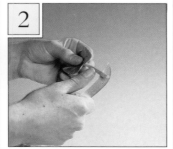

2

Clean any damage with sharp knife and trim leaf stem to 1–1½in (2.5–4cm).

3

Dip base of stem into hormone rooting powder, holding by leaf.

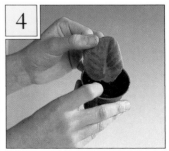

4

Gently insert in 2½in (6cm) pot ensuring leaf blade is not compressed or buried at all.

Remove leaf at base with sharp knife.

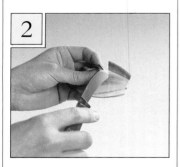

Cut leaf into 2in (5cm) pieces, cutting horizontally across leaf blade.

SANSEVIERIA TRIFASCIATA 'GOLDEN HAHNII'

This compact form of mother-in-law's tongue is a lower-growing variety which may be propagated from offsets or by leaf cuttings.

However, as the character of this variety could be adversely affected by splitting off offsets it is perhaps better to propagate by sections of leaves, even though this technique is certainly a great deal slower. Simply remove appropriate leaves with a sharp knife, taking care not to damage any other leaves and not to spoil the appearance of the mother plant. Cut the leaf horizontally to form 2in (5cm) pieces, and make sure you place them down the right way up to avoid propagating them upside down.

Dip the base of the cut leaf into hormone rooting powder and insert up to five or six cuttings in a 5½in (14cm) half-pot filled with cacti and succulent compost.

Keeping the compost barely moist, maintain a temperature of 68–70°F (20–21°C) in a well-lit situation. After several weeks, and perhaps even two or three months, each leaf should produce a new plantlet. When these are about 2in (5cm) tall, gently tease them out from the compost and pot up singly in a 2½in (6cm) pot filled with cacti and succulent compost, and grow on. When the plantlet is more mature, about three to six months old, the old leaf may be carefully removed with a sharp knife.

Take care not to invert pieces of leaf.

Dip base of cut surface into hormone rooting powder and insert five to six leaf pieces in a 5½in (14cm) half-pot.

SANSEVIERIA TRIFASCIATA 'LAURENTII'

*A*lthough, like *Sansevieria trifasciata* 'Hahnii', this variety of mother-in-law's tongue may be propagated from leaf cuttings (or rather sections of leaf cuttings) as well as from offsets, it is most unwise to propagate from sections of leaf. A plant successfully produced by this method will lack the yellow stripe that runs the length of the leaf on either side and will look far less interesting.

It is, therefore, preferable to propagate *Sansevieria trifasciata* 'Laurentii' from offsets. From late spring to midsummer, when the plant is capable of withstanding a certain amount of disturbance, remove it from its pot and, by a process of careful teasing and cutting, remove offsets that are about 8in (20cm) tall or at least about half of the size of the parent.

Pot up each piece in a 3½in (9cm) pot of cacti and succulent compost, taking care to plant the offset at a similar level at which it was growing. If the offset is rather wobbly, place a cane support in the pot until such time as the plant is stable enough without it.

Keep the offset in a well-lit position and do not overwater, rather trying to keep the compost barely moist and allowing it almost to dry out between waterings.

A stable temperature of 65–70°F (18–21°C) will help the offset to establish reasonably easily.

Gently remove plant from pot.

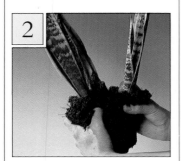

Carefully tease clumps apart to separate distinct plants.

Use sharp knife to cleanly cut and part the offset from the parent.

Dip base into hormone rooting powder and insert in 3½in (9cm) pot.

SAXIFRAGA STOLONIFERA

With the common name of mother of thousands this plant offers great potential for propagation. The mother plant produces long runners or stolons which dangle attractively over the side of the pot. In a similar way to a strawberry, the stolons form plantlets at the end of the runners and these may be propagated in two ways.

Propagation may be carried out from mid-spring to early autumn, earlier in the period being preferable if you wish to produce a reasonably sized plant in a shorter time.

The most successful method of propagation is to gently push the plantlet into the surface of the compost in a 3½in (9cm) pot filled with a peat-based potting compost. Within about a month rooting should have taken place and the stolon or runner may be carefully cut off at either end with a sharp pair of scissors.

Alternatively, plantlets up to about 2in (5cm) across may be cut from the runner and simply pushed gently into a 3½in (9cm) pot of seed and cutting compost. Transplant them once rooted. You may even be able to root them directly into a peat-based potting compost to save effort.

For either technique to be successful, keep the plantlet in moderate light, but out of direct light, at a temperature of 60–65°F (15–18°C). Keep the compost barely moist during the early stages of propagation, but increase the amount of water supplied as the plant starts actively to grow.

SCHEFFLERA ACTINOPHYLLA

The schefflera or umbrella plant may be propagated in mid- to late spring from seed, tip or stem cuttings.

If seed can be obtained it should be sown thinly in mid-spring in a tray or pan of seed and cutting compost, and germinated at about 68°F (20°C). Seedlings should be pricked out when large enough to handle, approximately 1–1½in (2.5–4cm), into a 2½in (6cm) pot of potting compost and grown on in good light.

Alternatively, tip or stem cuttings measuring 3–4in (7.5–10cm) should be removed with secateurs or pruning shears, dipped into hormone rooting powder and inserted one cutting per pot in a 2½–3½in (6–9cm) pot of seed and cutting compost.

Cover with a clear plastic bag and keep in reasonable light, but out of direct sunlight at a temperature of 70–75°F (21–24°C). The compost should be moist, but not too wet, to prevent rotting off.

After approximately one month, when rooting should have occurred and new growth should have started, the plastic bag may be removed and the plant weaned and grown on sufficiently until a well-formed root structure has been developed.

The plant may then be potted on in a 5in (13cm) pot of potting compost and staked, if necessary, to produce a straight-stemmed plant.

Remove 3–4in (7.5–10cm) tip cutting.

Dip base of stem into hormone rooting powder and insert in 2½–3½in (6–9cm) pot.

Cover cutting with clear plastic bag.

SEDUM RUBROTINCTUM

The attractive reddish-pink tinged succulent *Sedum rubrotinctum* is certainly one of the easiest succulents to propagate.

Although it may generally be propagated throughout the spring and summer, propagation is best carried out in mid- to late spring to enable the plant to develop freely through the summer months.

In order to propagate, simply select a stem of the sedum that is becoming rather long and cut off the top to produce a tip cutting of approximately 2in (5cm). Take particular care not to damage the plant or knock off too many of the fleshy leaves, making the plant look somewhat unsightly.

The tip cutting should be left for a couple of days to enable the base of the cutting to form a callus prior to being propagated. Surplus leaves at the base should also be pulled off from approximately ¾in (2cm) of the lower stem.

The base of the stem should then be dipped in hormone rooting powder and inserted in a 2½in (6cm) pot filled with cacti and succulent compost, having dibbled a small hole for the cutting first.

Place the cutting in a well-lit position at a temperature of about 65°F (18°C), keeping the compost barely moist. Within a few weeks the plant should have rooted and may be grown on as required.

SINNINGIA SPECIOSA

$\mathcal{C}$ommonly known as the gloxinia this spectacular, somewhat delicate plant may be propagated from leaf cuttings, division of the clump or from seed.

Commercially, plants are raised from seed and this method is probably the best technique to try, although plants can relatively easily be raised from leaf cuttings.

Division of the plant may be carried out in mid-spring, but this can be difficult as the plant is very fleshy and damage may easily be caused, resulting in a fungal infection which could cause subsequent loss.

Leaf cuttings taken in early summer should consist of healthy, developed leaves that are not too old or large. These should be carefully removed from the plant with a sharp knife, and the stem trimmed to a length of about 1½–2in (4–5cm). Once the base of the stem has been dipped in hormone rooting powder, the leaf may then be inserted in a 3½in (9cm) pot of peat-based potting compost.

The cutting should then be enclosed in a clear plastic bag and kept at 68–70°F (20–21°C) in reasonable light until rooted; this should take four to six weeks. A small tuber will then develop from which a plantlet will form. Grow on the plantlet, carefully weaning the plant out of its bag by gradually increasing the ventilation.

Leaf cuttings may also be propagated by inverting them on soft tissue and making clean cuts through the main veins. Where possible these should be reasonably spaced in four to six places. It is essential to use a very sharp knife or, even better, a scalpel. The leaf may then be turned up the right way and laid on a seed tray filled with seed and cutting compost that is just moist, gently placing the leaf on the surface to ensure that contact is made with the compost. Take care not to crush the tissue at any stage, otherwise rooting may occur. It may even be prudent to use a fungicidal spray of benomyl to help prevent rotting.

The leaf or leaves should then be enclosed within a clear plastic bag and kept at 68–70°F (20–21°C) for four to six weeks until rooted. Plantlets should then appear within a similar period; you should provide increased ventilation in the later stages to wean the plantlets. These may then be potted up singly in 3½in (9cm) pots of peat-based potting compost and grown on until large enough to pot into the final 5½in (14cm) half-pot in the same way as plantlets raised from leaf cuttings propagated by the first technique.

The gloxinia may also be raised from seed thinly sown onto seed and cutting compost in early to mid-spring. A 5½in (14cm) pan or small seed tray is ideal for this. Once sown, the seed should be covered with a piece of clear plastic or glass and kept at 70°F (21°C), ensuring that the compost remains moist. Germination should take about four weeks and may be patchy.

Once the seedlings are large enough to handle, probably after a further four to six weeks, they should be carefully weaned and then potted up singly in peat-based potting compost, in a 2½–3½in (6–9cm) pot first, and then later in a 5½in (14cm) half-pot.

Take care not to allow the compost to dry out at any time and also ensure that the plants are kept in a well-lit position out of direct sunlight.

SOLANUM CAPSICASTRUM

The Solanum capsicastrum or winter cherry may be propagated to flower and fruit within the same year and will provide a good display if started early. Seed may be collected from ripened fruits removed from a mature plant. When dry the seed should be sown thinly in a half-pot or pan or seed tray filled with seed and cutting compost. Lightly cover and keep at 70°F (21°C) until germinated, normally within two to three weeks, using a sheet of clear plastic, glass or a plastic bag. The compost should be kept evenly moist, but not too wet.

Once germinated, the cover should be removed and the seedlings grown on in a well-lit position, otherwise they will grow to be weak and leggy.

When large enough to handle at about 2in (5cm), they should be potted up singly in 3½in (9cm) pots of a peat-based potting compost and grown on at around 60°F (15°C), although they will adapt to temperatures above and below this, about 10°F (6°C) either way.

Grow on in a well-lit position with some light shade and pot up if required into a 4¼–5in (11–13cm) pot, again using a peat-based potting compost. Pinch out the top shoots, if necessary, to induce bushiness.

A key point to remember if you want to ensure that your plant produces fruit is either to grow it outside during the height of summer when it is in flower to enable insects to pollinate them or, alternatively, pollinate the flowers yourself, if you continue to grow the plant indoors. This may be easily achieved by lightly brushing the middle of the flower with an artist's brush.

SPATHIPHYLLUM WALLISII

*T*his plant is sometimes called white sails because of the beautiful white spathe which surrounds a white-to cream-coloured spadix commonly seen as the plant's flower.

The plant may be propagated with extreme care by division in mid- to late spring. Dense clumps may provide a number of new plants, but do not try to produce too many plants to the detriment of the parent.

Moisten the compost of the root ball well, and gently tease offsets of the main plant away, taking care to separate only those pieces with at least three to four leaves or more. Where there are less, try to ensure that these small plants are left attached to larger plants when separated.

Apart from teasing apart, use a sharp knife to sever the rhizome cleanly and try to keep as much root as possible attached to each potential new plant.

Pot up each piece in a 4¼in (11cm) pot of peat-based potting compost, or seed and cutting compost in which you may find plants will root more readily. Ensure that the plant is planted at the same level as it was when attached to the mother plant.

Support in the form of a cane may help to avoid root disturbance to large pieces in the early stages.

Covering the plant for a few weeks with a plastic bag may also help plants that have a small or damaged root system, removing it once the plant starts to produce new growth. After the division process treat all plants with great care and keep them at about 68–70°F (20–21°C) in moderate light, misting occasionally with tepid water, as the plant thrives in a reasonably humid environment.

Moisten compost thoroughly.

Carefully remove plant from pot.

Gently tease clump apart to separate pieces with more than four mature leaves.

Place new plant in 4¼in (11cm) pot.

Fill pot with peat-based potting compost taking care to avoid air spaces – but do not compact.

Gently firm to secure plant and water to settle compost.

STAPELIA VARIEGATA

The carrion flower, star flower or toad plant, is relatively easy to propagate from seed germinated in mid-spring at 68–70°F (20–21°C) in a 5½in (14cm) pan or seed tray of cacti and succulent compost. Seedlings will develop normally within a couple of weeks and, when large enough to handle at 1–1½in (2.5–4cm), may be potted up singly and grown on.

Alternatively, the plant may also be propagated by division or from cuttings.

As the plant grows it will become rather dense and overcrowded and the stems will begin to spill over the pot. This is probably a good time to consider repotting and propagating.

From late spring to mid-summer, at the time of repotting, gently tease away stems of the plant, where possible complete with roots. These should be potted up in a 2½–3½in (6–9cm) pot of cacti and succulent compost. Keep the compost barely moist and take particular care not to over-water, growing the plant in a well-lit position at about 68°F (20°C).

Cuttings may also be taken in early to mid-summer. These should be cut cleanly from the parent with a sharp knife, as close to the base as possible, particularly taking care not to damage the parent plant.

The cutting should then be left for a few days for the wound to dry and form a callus before being inserted gently in a 2½–3½in (6–9cm) pot of cacti and succulent compost. Hormone rooting powder may be used, if required, to help the rooting process. The cutting may then be treated in the same way as the plant propagated by division.

STEPHANOTIS FLORIBUNDA

It has to be said that the exquisitely scented stephanotis will either grow rampantly or will simply struggle, gradually losing its leaves. If you are lucky enough to be rewarded with the former then you should be able to propagate the plant; if not, then you are unlikely even to be able to produce material for propagation.

A healthy plant will produce a number of shoots which may be used to propagate from either after or before flowering. From mid-spring to early summer cut off tip cuttings up to 4in (10cm) with a sharp knife and insert one per 2½in (6cm) pot of seed and cutting compost, after having dipped the base of the stem in rooting powder.

Cover the cuttings with a clear plastic bag, keep the compost just moist, and place the cutting in a well-lit position, out of direct sunlight, at a temperature of 68–70°F (20–21°C). Rooting is slow and may take up to three months, after which the cover may be removed as soon as roots establish and new growth continues.

Two cuttings may then be planted in a 5in (13cm) pot of peat-based potting compost and grown around a wire hoop in opposite directions. Alternatively, two or three may be potted in a 7in (18cm) pot up a tall cane support, either way care being taken not to over-water, particularly in the early stages.

STRELITZIA REGINAE

*P*ropagation of the bird of paradise flower requires skill and also great patience.

The dark brown seeds with an orange tuft may be propagated, but take up to six months in a propagator at a temperature of around 75°F (24°C). Seedlings raised by this method may then be pricked out as they appear and are large enough to handle, taking care not to damage the brittle flesh root system. They should be potted up into 3½in (9cm) pots of peat-based potting compost and grown on in a well-lit position.

Alternatively, healthy mature plants may be divided in mid- to late spring, but really only if new plants can be easily identified and removed without causing too much damage to the parent or its offspring.

Moisten the compost and remove the plant from its pot. Carefully tease apart any new plant with three or four leaves or more. You will probably find this extremely difficult as the roots of the parent grow to become enormously thick, fleshy and quite tough. Nevertheless they are also subject to being easily damaged, which can then lead to rotting off.

Taking care to minimize the disturbance, pot up each new plant in an appropriate size of pot, probably 5–7in (13–18cm), using a peat-based potting compost. The next two to three months are crucial as the new plant produces a fresh root system. The plant should be kept at about 68°F (20°C) in a well-lit position out of direct sunlight, and the compost kept barely moist.

STREPTOCARPUS

*T*he cape primrose really is a most extraordinary plant which is fun to propagate.

Raised from seed sown at 70°F (21°C) in early to mid-spring, the plants should flower later in the summer. Alternatively, seed sown in late spring to early summer will produce a plant up to 4in (10cm) by the end of the growing season that will probably flower in the following spring.

In either case, sow thinly in a seed tray or 5½in (14cm) half-pot, pricking out when large enough singly into 3½in (9cm) pots of peat-based potting compost.

However, streptocarpus is far more interesting to raise from leaves, which can be done in various ways. Mature, but not old, leaves can be propagated as follows. They can be cut across the leaf to produce up to three or, possibly even four, pieces which may be inserted vertically in compost, inserting them to a depth of approximately ½in (1cm). The leaves may also be cut with a sharp knife along the midrib and the two halves inserted cut face down vertically in compost to a depth of approximately ½in (1cm).

Finally, a leaf may be laid onto the surface of compost, after having had several cuts made through the main veins from the underside.

For these three techniques use a seed tray filled with seed and cutting compost that is kept just moist at 68–70°F (20–21°C) in moderate light. New plants should appear within two months from the bottom of the cut pieces or from where the veins were cut.

Leave them until they are large enough to handle; at about 2in (5cm) they may be lifted, separated from the old leaf, potted up into 3½in (9cm) pots of peat-based potting compost, and grown on. During the propagation process you may find that covering the leaves with clear plastic produces better results – particularly when the leaf is laid on the surface. Watch out for any signs of rotting

SYNGONIUM PODOPHYLLUM

*S*yngonium may be propagated by the 'direct stick-ing' method. This is especially useful as the plant produces fleshy roots that are not very happy if disturbed, particularly in the early stages. From mid-spring to early summer 3–4in (7.5–10cm) tip cuttings should be cut cleanly from the plant with a sharp knife. Remove any lower leaves that would be buried when the cutting is inserted, again using a sharp knife for a clean wound.

The base of the cutting should then be dipped into hormone rooting powder and inserted three to a 3½in (9cm) pot of seed and cutting compost. Covering the cuttings with a clear plastic bag will not only help the cuttings to root faster, but may also encourage the production of aerial roots. Keep the plant in a reasonably lit position, out of direct sunlight, and maintain a temperature of 68–70°F (20–21°C) until rooted. This should be well within two months.

Keep the compost just moist until well rooted, when the bag can be removed and watering gradually increased as required. You may commence feeding with a dilute liquid fertilizer as soon as the plant starts actively to grow, at which time support in the form of a cane or moss pole may be given. Take care to remove any leaves that show signs of yellowing, or that are brown at the edges, before the rot spreads to other leaves. This is particularly important when the cuttings are enclosed within the plastic bag.

Remove 3–4in (7.5–10cm) tip cutting.

Dip base of stem into hormone rooting powder and insert three cuttings per 3½in (9cm) pot.

TOLMIEA MENZIESII

*T*he piggy-back plant or mother of thousands is another plant that lends itself well to being propagated readily. From mid-spring to late summer the plant may be propagated by either of two methods. Use whichever you find to be most successful.

The easiest way is to fill a 3½in (9cm) pot with seed and cutting compost and to place one of the leaves with an already formed young plantlet onto the surface of the compost. Do not cut the leaf from the mother plant, but leave it attached. Ensure that the leaf stays in contact with the compost by anchoring it down with a long-shanked staple or opened-up paper clip to secure the stem close to the leaf.

Rooting should occur within a month, after which the new plant may be separated from the mother plant with a sharp pair of scissors. Leave the young plant to develop a little more before removing the clip and, if required, the old leaf which can simply be carefully cut off.

Another way of propagating tolmiea is to cut off plantlet-bearing leaves, complete with 1–1¼in (2.5–3cm) of stem. The leaf stalk should then be inserted in a 3½in (9cm) pot of seed and cutting compost, taking care to ensure that the base of the leaf is in contact with the surface of the compost. The plantlet should root within a month.

Whichever way you choose to propagate the plant, ensure that the compost is kept just moist and not too wet, and that the plantlet is provided with a well-lit position out of direct sunlight, at least for the first few weeks. Tolmiea should root well at 65–68°F (18–20°C). Once rooted, it should be grown on and fed with a liquid fertilizer before being finally potted up into a 5½in (14cm) half-pot of potting compost.

1

Select leaf with plantlet already formed.

2

Place on 3½in (9cm) pot filled with seed and cutting compost, using paper-clip to secure stem.

3

Gently press paper-clip over stem to anchor plant to surface of compost.

4

Leave attached to plant until rooted when stem can be severed.

TRADESCANTIA

*T*radescantia can be rooted readily in compost or water, using whichever method you find to be the most successful.

This plant tends to grow quite lank and should be renewed or pinched back regularly, especially from mid-spring to late summer, when not only can the mother plant be allowed to re-generate, but the 'trimmings' may be used as propagation material.

Pinch off, or cut with a sharp knife, tip cuttings up to 3in (7.5cm) in length, ensuring that the base of the stem is cut cleanly and not crushed to avoid any likelihood of disease.

Insert five cuttings in a 3½in (9cm) pot of seed and cutting compost and keep at 65°F (18°C) in a well-lit position out of direct sunlight. Maintain the compost at just moist, taking care to ensure that it does not become too wet.

Within two or three weeks roots should have been produced, and the plant can be grown on with further water and liquid fertilizer added as required.

Cuttings may also be rooted in water, in similar conditions to those rooted conventionally. When the roots have grown to approximately 1½–2in (4–5cm) in length they may then be potted up five to a 3½in (9cm) pot of potting compost and grown on accordingly.

1

Remove 3in (7.5cm) tip cuttings.

2

Gently insert in 3½in (9cm) pot of seed and cutting compost.

3

Insert five cuttings per pot taking care not to crush stems or leaves.

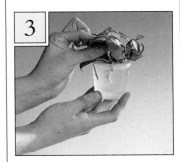

3

Instead of inserting in compost simply insert directly into rooting gel or water.

V

VRIESIA SPLENDENS

Commercially, the *Vriesia splendens* or flaming sword is propagated from seed.

Propagation by seed in the home requires a temperature of up to 80°F (27°C) in order to encourage the seed to germinate. Seed should be sown very thinly onto the surface of seed and cutting compost in a small seed tray, half-pot or pan. The compost should be kept moist and the seed germinated under clear plastic, glass or a plastic bag.

If the temperature is maintained at up to 80°F (27°C) germination should start to occur after two to three weeks. Continue to grow on the seedlings at a similar high humidity level, but you may lower the temperature to 75°F (24°C), and then to 70°F (21°C) after a few weeks. When the seedlings have about six to eight leaves, gently prick them out one per 2½in (6cm) pot, using a specialized bromeliad compost or peat-based potting compost.

Vriesia also produces offsets from the base of the plant after the mother plant has flowered. These may be removed from mid-spring to mid-summer by moistening the compost and gently teasing the offset away from the mother. Use a sharp knife, if necessary, to avoid any damage.

Offsets should be at least 4–6in (10–15cm) before being separated to grow on their own. Once separated, they should be planted one per pot in a 3½in (9cm) pot of bromeliad or peat-based potting compost. Cover the offset with a clear plastic bag to encourage establishment and keep it in moderate light at about 68°F (20°C) for up to two months to be sure that it roots sufficiently well.

After this period gradually wean the offset to grow on, on its own.

These methods may be applied to most species of vriesia, although some varieties do not produce offsets. Where offsets are not produced from the base of the plant, but appear out of the space between the leaf and the main stem (leaf axil), they should not be removed, but should be left to carry on growing.

Carefully saw stem into 4–8in (10–20cm) pieces.

Taking care to keep stem the right way up, dust base in hormone rooting powder.

Insert stem in 4¼–5in (11–13cm) pot.

Firm compost around stem, ensuring that at least one third of stem is below compost surface.

YUCCA ELEPHANTIPES

The yucca has become a popular houseplant and may be propagated from offsets, quite different to how the commercial grower propagates it.

If you wish to emulate the commercial grower you will need a pruning saw to cut the stem into 4–8in (10–20cm) pieces and a fair deal of strength. Also take care to avoid any accidents!

The thick pieces of stem can be rooted after having been dipped into hormone rooting powder and inserted in an appropriate size of pot, probably 4¼–5in (11–13cm), filled with seed and cutting compost.

Within a couple of months or so of being kept in reasonable light at 70°F (21°C), with the compost kept just moist, the stem should root and new shoots should make their appearance. If you do use this technique, apart from taking great care, also be sure to make the stem so that you insert it in the compost the right way up!

Probably a more reasonable method is to remove offsets when they are up to 8in (20cm) long; ideally they should not be shorter than 6in (15cm). In mid-spring the offsets may be cut with a very sharp knife at the bottom of the potential new plant where it joins the main stem.

Hormone rooting powder may be used to dip the base of the offset in prior to it being inserted in a 3½–4¼in (9–11cm) pot of seed and cutting compost. Keep the compost just moist, and maintain a temperature of around 70°F (21°C). The offset should be kept in a reasonably well-lit position, but out of direct sunlight.

After about two months the offset should have rooted sufficiently and new growth started, at which time the watering may be increased, but still allow the compost almost to dry out between waterings. Feeding with a liquid fertilizer may also be commenced, and as soon as the plant is large enough it can be potted up into a 4¼–5in (11–13cm) pot of peat-based potting compost taking great care not to overpot.

INDEX

■ PICTURE CREDITS AND ■ ACKNOWLEDGEMENTS

The author and publishers would like to thank Stuart Low for providing plants for photography, and Camden Garden Centre for the loan of propagation equipment.

Andrew Sydenham pp 8, 10; George Ward Ltd p 9; Fison's Horticultural Division p 15br; Eric Crichton Photos pp 221, 39, 401, 42, 46, 70, 80, 921, 109; Michael Warren, Photos Horticultural pp 25r, 30r, 92r, 1051; Ian Howes pp 22r, 23r, 24, 271, 29, 31, 37, 38, 40r, 43, 44, 50, 51, 54, 56, 57, 59, 62, 64, 65, 66, 67, 84, 85, 86, 87, 88, 97, 99, 100, 101, 1141, 116, 119r, 120; Holly Gate International Ltd pp 27r, 64, 79, 94, 1191; Peter Stiles pp 231, 251, 53, 68, 811, 105r, 115; Trevor Wood p 78

All other photographs by Paul Forrester.
Illustrations by Lorraine Harrison.